365 Ways to Live Green

for KiDS
Saving the Environment at Home, School, or at Play—Every Day!

By **Sheri Amsel**

Published by
Adams Media, a division of F+W Media, Inc.
57 Littlefield Street, Avon, MA 02322. U.S.A.
www.adamsmedia.com

ISBN 10: 1-60550-634-6
ISBN 13: 978-1-60550-634-0

Contains material adapted and abridged from *The Everything® Kids' Environment Book*
by Sheri Amsel, copyright © 2008 by F+W Media, Inc.,
ISBN 10: 1-59869-670-X, ISBN 13: 978-1-59869-670-7.

Printed in Canada

JIHGFEDCBA

Library of Congress Cataloging-in-Publication Data
is available from the publisher.

This publication is designed to provide accurate and authoritative information with regard to the
subject matter covered. It is sold with the understanding that the publisher is not engaged in
rendering legal, accounting, or other professional advice. If legal advice or other expert assistance
is required, the services of a competent professional person should be sought.
—From a *Declaration of Principles* jointly adopted by a Committee of the American Bar Association
and a Committee of Publishers and Associations

Many of the designations used by manufacturers and sellers to distinguish their product are
claimed as trademarks. Where those designations appear in this book and Adams Media was
aware of a trademark claim, the designations have been printed with initial capital letters.

The pages of this book are printed on 100% post-consumer recycled paper.

*This book is available at quantity discounts for bulk purchases.
For information, please call 1-800-289-0963.*

Contents

contents

CHAPTER 3
FIGHT POLLUTION!...75

contents

CHAPTER 4
ANIMALS...101

contents

CHAPTER 8
AT HOME, AT SCHOOL, AND BEYOND...175

contents

365 Ways to Live Green for kids

Introduction

Congratulations on getting this book! You are about to set off on an adventure to save the planet. Your adventure will last more than 365 days—it will last a lifetime!

This book has lots of fun facts and stories about the environment, as well as games you can play with your friends, activities you can do on your own or with your family, and special projects that will help make our planet a cleaner, better place.

Best of all, when you share what you learn with other people, you help spread the word of how important it is to "go green." All kinds of people can learn from your example and the good work that you do.

So when you learn something new from this book or find a new way to go green, tell your teacher, your parents, your family, and your friends what you have learned and invite them to do projects with you. We are all part of the same world, and when we work together, we can do great things!

Our planet is a special place. Even when you do something that appears small—recycling cans or paper, reusing something instead of throwing it away, or turning off the water while you brush your teeth—you are helping keep the planet clean and healthy. Some of the projects or activities in this book are big, and some are small. Doing any one of them will help the earth and make you a greener person!

Remember that every great journey starts with a single step. Deciding to "go green" is a decision we make with every new day, and even the smallest choice to recycle, reuse and reduce goes a very long way. You can do it!

So start reading! Saving the planet is fun!

CHAPTER 1

FOOD FOR THOUGHT

1 RETHINK YOUR "ENVIRONMENT"

What is the environment? The answer may surprise you. The environment is all living and nonliving things on Earth. Your indoor environment includes your family, pets, and houseplants, but it also includes the furniture, floors, windows, and even the air temperature around you! Outside, your environment becomes the trees, grass, insects, birds, clouds, wind, and ground. Environments can be big: as big as an entire planet—or small: smaller than you can see. If you are a beetle, your environment could be a rotten log or a garden. If you are a lake trout your environment is the sand, rocks, ducks, water striders, and the very water you live in.

The first step to going green is to know, understand, and appreciate that you are part of many environments, big and small. Your actions have an effect on those environments: some actions can promote the health of the environment, and some actions do not.

It's important that you realize that your actions *do* make a difference in the health of the environment.

2 NAME THAT ENVIRONMENT!

Sit in a circle with friends or your family and take turns naming an animal or plant. Then the person to your right has to name five to ten traits of the environment of that suggested animal or plant. For example, if they say: "cactus," you might say: "sand, heat, lizard, tortoise, rocks, rattlesnake, wind, scorpion, vulture, roadrunner." You may learn something new!

3 DRAW THE ENVIRONMENT

Find pictures of animals in old magazines and trace them (or cut them out and paste them) onto the center of a large sheet of paper. You could also look up images on the Internet: get your parent to help you, if need be, to find images and print them out. Now draw the animals' environment around them. For example, if you have traced an African elephant, add the grassy savannah. Add a baobab tree and a bright blue sky. Add a herd of zebras and a giraffe. This is an elephant environment! Make the drawing as big as you like to make room for a big environment. And don't just do land animals: try doing this exercise with aquatic life or insects. Choose animals or organisms you've never heard of before, so the exercise will help you learn lots of cool stuff. If you do several animals or organisms in the same geographical environment, maybe you can get a large piece of poster board and make a collage! Think big!

4 DESCRIBE YOUR ENVIRONMENT

You are part of the environment, too. What is your habitat like? What is your diet like? Imagine if a biologist or scientist described you as an animal, and made a detailed study of your habits, your features, and how you relate to your environment. You may learn a thing or two about yourself if you take a step back and describe yourself as you would an animal or an organism! Don't leave out how you relate to other "creatures" in your environment, and how many resources you use as part of your daily life.

Consider this: What about your environment could change? For example, could you change your diet? Could you change how much you eat or drink? Think about how you relate to other animals, organisms, or people in your environment: how could that change? What effect do you think it would have?

Often, when people think about changing their habits or their lifestyle, they think about themselves in isolation. They think:

"I'm changing this about me because it's what I want." Once you describe your environment and see your relationship to everyone and everything in it, maybe you'll think of changes you could make because it's what your *environment* wants, or what would benefit the world around you.

5 MAKE A LIST OF CARNIVORES

Carnivores are meat-eating animals. Carnivores can also refer to the order of mammals that contains bears, wolves, cats, weasels, seals, etc. Can you think of other animals that eat meat? Human beings are very special in the animal kingdom because we can choose how much meat we eat, and we can even choose to eat no meat at all. People who do not eat meat are called vegetarians. We will learn more about them and vegetarian choices later.

The companies that produce and package meat for human consumption take steps to make sure that the meat is safe to eat, and free of unhealthy bacteria. Sometimes, though, their best efforts do not or cannot prevent instances in which meat becomes "tainted," or affected by harmful bacteria or organisms. When tainted food is discovered, the companies work together with business owners and local government to make sure that none of this harmful food is available for sale. They take it all back and dispose of it properly: this is called a "recall."

Information about food recalls is broadcast on the television news and is printed in the newspaper because it is important for people to know. Even supermarkets put up signs to let people know about recalls.

Information about recalls is available on the Internet, too. If you're interested in learning more about recalls and how you can make sure your food is clean and safe to eat, talk to your parents about ways to obtain more information.

6 MAKE A LIST OF HERBIVORES

The herbivores are plant-eating animals. If you or someone you know is a vegetarian, that's a kind of herbivore, too! Make a list of herbivores. Use your local library to help find answers.

And where would the human herbivores in your area eat? Look up vegetarian restaurants in your phone book or on the Internet: maybe there are more than you thought, or there are fewer than you hoped!

As part of your research into herbivores, you may be surprised to learn how many plants can be eaten, or are "edible." In fact, by learning about plants and vegetables, you can learn a lot about a country, a culture, and human history in general. For example, when bacteria ruined potato crops in Ireland in the nineteenth century, the Irish people found themselves unable to farm and eat a plant that was essential to their survival. Tens of thousands of Irish people had to leave the country to find food and jobs. Some of those people may even be ancestors of yours!

And you thought potatoes were boring. Research plants and herbivores, and be surprised at how much you learn!

7 CALLING ALL INSECTIVORES!

Insectivorous plants are plants that trap and digest insects as added food. Surely you can name one such plant: its name sounds like it's from outer space! Make a list of insectivores and see if any are available for purchase at your local nursery.

Did you know that some people eat insects? Some cultures and countries consider certain kinds of insects a good source of protein; in other places, bugs like ants, grasshoppers and bees are considered delicacies when prepared a certain way. Other cultures may fry the insects or even dip them in chocolate. Before you say "yuck," bear in mind: you never know until you try it!

8 LEARN ABOUT: INSECT-EATING PLANTS

Pitcher plants trap insects by having a sweet smell and have red lines running inside like a runway. Insects follow the lines down into the pitcher looking for nectar. When they try to get out, they find stiff hairs pointing down, blocking their escape. Soon they get tired and fall into the acidic liquid in the bottom of the pitcher where they dissolve over time.

Sundews have sticky fluid on their hairy leaves that insects mistake for nectar. When an insect lands on the leaf it gets stuck. The leaf rolls up with the insect inside and dissolves it.

Venus flytraps have a really cool adaptation for catching insects. At the end of each leaf stalk is a clamshell-shaped leaf that lies open with a red-colored inside to attract insects. An insect landing inside the leaf will trip a hair trigger that snaps the clamshell closed. The insect, now trapped inside, gets dissolved by the plant and absorbed as food.

9 NAME SOME OMNIVORES

Omnivores are animals that eat both meat and plant matter. The prefix "omni-" means "all." Naming all the omnivores would make a long list! If you eat meat and vegetables, guess what that makes you! Research and name other omnivores, and consider what relationship these creatures have with their environment, if they eat everything!

10 STUDY THE HUMAN DIET

Do some research into all the different kinds of things humans eat and drink. It is very interesting to read about other cultures and see what their diets are. Read about people in China, or Africa, or North America, and compare and contrast their diets. What do their diets say about them? Which countries have health problems related to their diets? This is an important environmental issue, because living organisms are part of our environment, and people's diets have a profound effect on the earth, its plants, and its animals.

One interesting approach to take is to find out where the average person in a given area gets his or her calories. For example, how many of their daily calories come from food, and how many from drink? How many calories come from sugar? How many calories come from vegetables, or from meats? Each one of these statistics is very revealing about people and their diets.

One very interesting aspect of the human diet, in addition to what people eat, is how food is preserved and prepared. Do some research! Some foods, you'll find, are frozen, while others are preserved by chemical additives. The more you learn about food, the more you learn about yourself and your own body. After all, you are what you eat!

11 TRY A DIFFERENT CUISINE

As part of your research into the varied human diet, ask your parents to take you to a restaurant with a cuisine you have never tried before: it could be Mexican, Chinese, Indian, Ethiopian, Korean, Japanese . . . depending on where you live, you may have a hard time choosing! Once you are there, try new foods. See how other human animals like yourself eat!

Don't be shy about talking to the waiter or waitress and saying, "This is my first time eating this kind of food." Describe to the waiter or waitress what kind of food you usually like to eat: whether or not it contains meat, whether it's salty or sweet, whether it's hot or cold. Then ask your server's opinion as to what you might like, based on your own food preferences. The server should be more than happy to describe the foods to you and make sure you are happy because they want you to come back and eat there again. Your parents will probably be so happy that you are trying new things, they'll buy you dessert!

12 DO RESEARCH ON: ORGANIC FARMING

Organic foods are fruits, vegetables, grains, and dairy products that are grown without using chemicals such as manmade pesticides and fertilizers. To be called organic, food cannot have chemicals added to it later or be exposed to radiation (food manufacturers sometimes do this to oils and other foods to keep them from going bad while they wait on store shelves to be sold). To be considered organic, plants themselves also can't be genetically altered. Organic meat comes from animals that have had no hormones or antibiotics.

People like organic foods because they consider them more pure, healthy, and tasty. With no additives there is no chance that you will be eating chemicals that you don't want in your body. The National Research Council (NRC) has found through a study that children and babies take in the pesticides found on the foods they eat and the pesticides build up in their bodies. A study by the U.S. Department of Agriculture found that pesticides stayed on fruits and vegetables after they'd been washed and even peeled! To protect their kids and themselves from this, many people eat only organic foods.

Organic farms usually have lots of things for sale to help generate funds to stay in business. Take a good look around the farm stand of your local farms, if they have one: you may find different kinds of honey, or jams and preserves, or even salsas made with organic tomatoes. The farms may sell clothing, too, made from environmentally friendly products and fabrics. Don't leave the store without finding at least three vegetables or products that you've never heard of before: find out how people usually prepare and eat them. Try new things! It's a big environment out there!

13 DO AN ORGANIC TASTE TEST

Do foods grown organically taste better then foods grown with chemicals? You can do a test to find out. You will need to go to your local food co op and buy a few things. Try a few organic foods like an apple, cheddar cheese, and carrots. Now buy the same foods from your grocery store. Make sure they are not organic. (Most stores have special displays for their organic foods.) You will need some taste-testing volunteers and a grownup to help you cut up the food.

Have a paper and pencil to write down the comments from each taste tester about the foods they tried.

1. Have them each taste a slice of apple. Do not tell them if it is organic or not!

2. Give them each a sip of water. Then have them each taste a slice of the other kind of apple.

3. Ask them which tasted better and why. Write down their responses.

4. Try this with all the foods you bought.

5. Afterward, see how the comments rated the organic food compared to the chemically treated food. What did you find out?

14 SPREAD THE WORD: ORGANIC IS GREEN!

Many people think that growing foods organically is better for the environment. Farms that grow organic foods have no chemicals running off their land into lakes and streams. Birds that land in organic farm fields are not exposed to chemical pesticides. Butterflies and honeybees can live on or near organic farms without being killed accidentally by pesticides meant for farm pests. Even the people who work on organic farms have a healthier environment. Exposure to pesticides can make farm workers feel sick, and over a long period of time can make them very ill. According to the World Health Organization, 3 million people are poisoned every year by pesticides and 220,000 of them die. About 10 percent of the 70,000 chemicals used in the United States can cause cancer. The use of chemical pesticides should at least make people wonder. Even better, it should make you think about alternatives you might use that are safer for the environment.

15 READ THE RULES ABOUT ORGANIC

The Organic Food Production Act was passed in the United States in 1990 and calls for the United States Department of Agriculture (USDA) to make national standards for organic products. The law says any product that is labeled "organic" must be raised without synthetic chemicals or in ground that has not been treated with chemicals for at least three years.

Labels on foods can be interesting to read. Take time to sit and read them. Compare one label to another. See if one cereal has more sugar than another. If a product says "natural" on its front, look at its ingredients to see if there are any chemicals or preservatives. Does the organic product have more calories or sodium (salt) than the nonorganic product? If so, why? The more questions you ask, the more you learn.

16 UNDERSTAND WHY SOME PEOPLE USE PESTICIDES

The reason many farms use pesticides and fertilizers is that people think they make food easier to grow. Farmers lose less food to pests and they can add nutrients to the ground that are lost from growing crop after crop, year after year. Organic foods are more expensive to buy, partly because there are less of them available. As people ask for more and more organic foods, more will be raised and sold. Hopefully over time we will find organic foods everywhere.

Does your family use pesticides in your gardens or on your lawn? Start a conversation with your parents and you may find that you don't need to use some pesticides, but that other pesticides are necessary to keep your lawn and your gardens green and healthy. Once you start talking about why and how you use pesticides, you can begin to think about organic ways to treat the environment closest to your own home. Find out if there are any lawn care companies in your area that specialize in organic products. Do organic products always work the same or better than chemicals? What's the difference between the products? Maybe you can find a lawn or garden in your community that is organic, and you can compare and contrast it with a lawn or garden that uses chemicals. Make note of your findings and share them with your parents.

17 RID PESTS THE ORGANIC WAY!

Scientists have come up with some pretty cool ways to kill pests without using chemicals. One way is called a "pheromone trap." That is when they make a sticky trap that smells like the insects themselves. This attracts insects inside, where they become stuck and die. Organic farmers can place pheromone traps all over their fields to trap and kill insects without using chemicals.

18 MEMORIZE THIS: FOOD WEB

A food web is the interconnecting food chains of who eats whom in a natural habitat. A food web can be a very fragile and sensitive thing: If you remove one organism from a food web, the other organisms are going to have to find something else to eat, and If you introduce a new organism into a food web, you may have more than one organism competing for the same limited supply of food!

19 PLAY ENVIRONMENTAL TAG

Get together with a few friends and have each of your friends choose an organism to be. You can be a plant, an herbivore (an animal that eats only plants), a carnivore (an animal that eats meat), or an omnivore (an animal that eats everything). The herbivores can chase the plants.

The carnivores can chase the herbivores. The omnivores can chase the plants and herbivores. Run around and have fun being your own food web!

20 LEARN THIS ECO-TERM: PHOTOSYNTHESIS

Photosynthesis is the process of green plants making food from water, carbon dioxide, and the energy of the sun.

Do some research into photosynthesis and learn what interferes with the process, or makes it more difficult. If you learn what interferes with photosynthesis, you can take steps to fix the situation!

21 GET TO KNOW: DECOMPOSERS

Every living thing on Earth needs energy to live. Not all organisms get it the same way. Only plants can make their own energy through photosynthesis. Animals must eat plants or other animals to survive. When animals and plants die, their bodies decompose and release their nutrients back into the environment. The nutrients they release when they decompose can be used to nourish new plants. They also nourish decomposers. Decomposers include insects, bacteria, fungi, and other microorganisms. All these animals and plants are part of the energy cycle.

22 SUBSTITUTE SOY

Americans (especially kids) are big consumers of fast food! But most fast foods are full of fat, excess calories, and cost a lot. The fast food industry also buys a lot of beef from Brazil where rainforests are being stripped to make room for more beef cattle. Next time you have a craving for fast food, have a soy burger or soy hot dog instead. Soy is made from the plant matter of the soybean and tastes similar to the meats you might already enjoy eating. You never know, you might love it!

23 COOK WITH TOFU

Tofu is a solid form of soybeans and is high in protein, something humans need for good nutrition. Look for a tofu cookbook in the bookstore or the library and see how versatile this healthy alternative to meat is! On its own, tofu does not have much flavor, but that's what makes it such a versatile and fun food. For example, if you put tofu into your spaghetti sauce as a substitute for meat the tofu will take on the flavors of your sauce. You can also cook tofu with oil, vegetables, and spices and make a tasty stir fry! If you go to the organic or "health food" section of your supermarket, you will find blocks of tofu—ranging from very soft to extra firm—and you will also find lots of products that contain tofu. These products are flavored and spiced so that they taste good: there are "chicken nuggets" that are made with tofu, and even a tofu turkey for Thanksgiving! Although using tofu may sound new and strange, tofu is essentially soybeans, and one of the places where they grow the most·soybeans is the state of Wisconsin! In other words, tofu is as American as you can get!

24 TRY GOING VEGGIE!

If your parents are always telling you to eat your vegetables, turn the conversation around and talk to them about trying vegetarianism. You could try it for a day, or a week, or a month: it's up to you and your family! There are several different kinds of vegetarians, and many people choose to be vegetarian as a way of being closer to the products of the earth and not contributing to the industry that uses lots of resources to make food out of animals. Basically, a vegetarian is someone who does not eat meat, chicken, or seafood. A vegan (VEEG-un) is someone who does not eat animal products of any kind, including milk, honey, and eggs.

Remember that before you make any change to your diet, you need to discuss it with your parents and your doctor, because the most important thing about your diet is that you get the nutrition you need to grow. You can make good nutrition choices as a vegetarian, but do some research first. Maybe there is a friend or family member who is already a vegetarian who you can talk to.

Earlier, we talked about reading food labels and paying attention to how foods are prepared. You may think that eating French fries at a fast food restaurant is vegetarian because potatoes are vegetables, but did you know that some people cook French fries in oils and fluids that contain beef? And that vegetarian soup on the menu: did the chef make it with chicken stock? Some restaurants may think that being a vegetarian means that you don't eat red meat but you do eat chicken and seafood, so it's always best to ask.

Some vegetarians and vegans object to the use of animals for any human purpose, including using animals in scientific experiments and using animals to make clothing. There are many different kinds of vegetarians, and many people who define the word differently. If you're considering vegetarianism, you can decide for yourself what you oppose and what you support. The important thing is to be informed.

25 UNDERSTAND: COMPOSTS

Compost is rotting organic matter, like grass clippings, leaves, vegetable scraps, and bits of wood and straw. After it is finished decomposing it can be used to fertilize your garden. When mixed with some soil, the bacteria, fungi, worms, and insects that live in a compost pile will break down all the rotting matter, releasing the nutrients. This creates a rich fertilizer material that you can add to your garden to help plants grow. Composting is something that anyone can do. Besides making great fertilizer, it is a good way to get rid of garden waste without filling up our landfills.

26 WORD UP!: PRODUCERS

The producers are at the bottom of the food chain, making their own food through photosynthesis and providing food for all the herbivores (plant-eating animals).

27 MAKE YOUR OWN COMPOST

Use a plastic garbage can that can sit in your backyard. Or just make a pile in a corner of your yard. You can add vegetable kitchen scraps, eggs shells, and coffee grounds. Don't add any meat scraps. A mixture of different organic material including grass, leaves, and food scraps creates the best compost. Add some plain dirt to the mixture now and then, if you have some available. Decomposing compost needs air, so the pile (or the garbage can) will have to be stirred with a shovel every time you add more materials. It will get hot when it is decomposing. If it doesn't rain you may have to water your compost a little to keep it moist (but not too wet—or it will mold). When it is ready—after it has transformed into a rich, dark, earthy material—add it to your garden. Your plants will love it!

28 DO THE COMPOST TEST

Make some compost this winter in a small tub or pile in your yard. Follow these instructions for a successful compost mix. You know your compost is ready when it is dark and earthy, like the inside of a chocolate cake. In the spring, dig a spot in your yard for a garden, or use an existing garden spot or two big clay pots on your porch. You will need two spots of about the same size. They can be small for this test, just one to two square feet. You'll need a garden shovel and flower seeds (or two small flowering plants of about the same size from a nursery).

1. Use your garden shovel and loosen up the soil in your two garden spots. If you are using two pots, fill both of them with soil right from your yard.
2. In one spot (or one pot), mix in some of the dark compost. Mix it up well with your shovel.
3. Now plant seeds (or a flowering plant) in each spot. Water them well.
4. Over the next few weeks, keep both spots equally watered and weeded.
5. After a few weeks do you notice a difference in how the seeds or plants are doing? Which one is doing better? Can you explain this difference?

29 EAT LIKE A WORM!

Make a model of an earthworm's environment, and a great party dessert, too!

1. Pour 2 cups of cold milk into a large bowl.
2. Add 1 package of chocolate-flavored instant pudding and pie filling.
3. Beat with a whisk until well mixed.

4. Stir in one 8-ounce tub of whipped topping.

5. Then stir in 1 cup crushed chocolate sandwich cookies.

6. Divide mixture into ten clear, plastic cups.

7. Sprinkle more crushed chocolate sandwich cookies on top.

8. Keep cold in the fridge.

9. Right before serving, push a gummy worm into each cup.

You can also find variations on this recipe, using ice cream instead of pudding. Be creative! Take a look at some things you might want to mix in with ice cream, and see if they look like something else outside of your house!

30 SHARE THIS ECO-STORY: DUMPS

When people started farming about 10,000 years ago, they gave up their wandering, hunting and gathering lives. With all those people living in one place for a long time, they started to build up a lot of garbage. This was how the first garbage dumps were born. People have been making garbage dumps for as long as they have been living in one place. Even Native Americans from thousands of years ago, after a big buffalo hunt, would leave behind a pile of garbage that was as big as some dumps today. It is believed that as early as 500 B.C., the Greeks were creating dumps outside of their cities. Amazingly, many of those ancient dumps are now important archeological sites!

You can learn a lot about a people from what is in their garbage dumps. The first settlers in America dealt with their garbage by dumping it over their back fence, in the river, or by burying it in their yards. They often burned garbage as well. Then, as communities grew into towns, they made town dumps. Now we call garbage dumps "landfills." Sadly, many early landfills were made in wetlands, which were thought to be wasteland back then. Early landfills leaked into rivers and lakes. They used to catch fire and even explode sometimes, because as garbage rots, it gives off methane, a flammable gas. The first garbage-burning plant in the United States, called an "incinerator," was built on Governor's Island in New York in 1885. By 1914, there were 300 incinerators burning garbage in the United States.

31 DO RESEARCH ON: LANDFILLS

Landfills have changed a lot from the first city dump. As of 1995, there were more than 2,500 landfills in the United States. In 1993, a law was passed that all landfills must be lined with a big plastic liner to keep them from leaking into the environment. They also have to have "gas monitors" to keep track of the dangerous gases that build up. Researchers have found that each American generates about 4.5 pounds of garage every day. The United States makes more garbage than any other country on the planet. We have 5 percent of the people on Earth, but make almost one-third of the entire world's garbage! So as landfills keep filling up, people will have to find more places for all that trash. In the future, landfills will be buried, landscaped, and reclaimed into golf courses or city parks all over America.

32 SHARE THIS ECO-FACT: GARBAGE

In the years 1347–1351, the bubonic plague, also called the "black death," or simply "the plague" spread through Europe, Asia and Africa, killing 75 million people. What they didn't know at the time was that it was all caused by too much garbage in the streets! Piles of garbage attracted rats, which had fleas, which carried the disease. The rats carried the plague from place to place. The lack of sanitation made the spread of the plague the worst in human history.

33 KNOW THIS: TOXIC WASTE

Toxic waste is trash that can harm or kill living things, including people. It often consists of chemicals, but can be medical waste too, such as discarded needles or latex gloves. Toxic waste is very harmful to the environment because it can pollute rivers and streams so badly that fish can't live there anymore. It can pollute the land so badly that no one can plant vegetables or even put a house there anymore.

One of the suggestions later in this book is to organize a group of people to pick up litter on the beach or in the woods or in a park. One thing you should always remember is that pollution of this kind may be dangerous to touch. This is why you should wear work gloves or use a "litter stick" (you will learn how to make one, later in this book). You should also go litter picking with an adult, in case you come across something like a medical needle or something that looks or smells funny. You want the environment to be safe, but you want to keep yourself safe, first!

34 GO ON A HOME TOXIC HUNT

It is very important that you do this exercise with an adult, such as one of your parents. Tell them that you want to research what things in your house are potentially toxic, to make sure everything is stored safely and securely. Your parent can lead you around the house and show you where you might find such items. Bring a pad of paper and make notes. Ask questions, and be sure that containers of toxic matter like cleansers, paints and poisons are closed tight, out of reach of small children, and are stored, when necessary, behind a locked or bolted door. It is also very important to keep these materials away from your pet, especially if you have a dog who likes to nose around and get into things! Your parent may also show you the phone number to call, in case of an emergency related to toxins. (Note, too, that there is a different set of actions to take if your pet swallows anything poisonous.)

By doing this exercise, you are helping to keep your family safe while at the same time educating yourself about an important part of your environment. But remember: Do not do this alone. Always be with a parent.

35 WORD UP!: GENES

Genes are the smallest unit of heredity. We have more than 20,000 genes that map out all of our traits, from the color of our eyes to the shape of our earlobes. Genes are what make us different from everyone around us. Our parents pass on certain genes to us—and their parents passed on others to them!

36 TEACH YOURSELF ABOUT: GENETIC ENGINEERING

Everything about us, from the color of our eyes and hair to our height, is mapped out in our genes. The same holds true for plants. The fruits and vegetables that we grow have genes, too. That is what makes an apple red or green, sweet or sour, crispy or soft. We can alter those genes if we want a special kind of trait, such as sweeter taste. Farmers have been doing this for hundreds of years. Instead of letting their plants be pollinated by the bees, the farmer takes the pollen from a plant with sweeter fruit and uses it to pollinate the plant with better color. After a while they get the fruit they want and begin growing a tree that is consistently sweet and good-looking. A new kind of apple has been made! This is a form of genetic engineering.

37 **D**O RESEARCH ON: GM FOO**D**

Food scientists have taken this a step further by adding genes to plants in the laboratory to give them the traits they want. They can add genes that keep plants from growing moldy in the field or that allow them to survive dry weather. They can even be altered to kill the insect pests that eat them. Scientists have also added vitamins to plants, like rice, so when people grow them they get more vitamins from their food.

The good side of GM food (genetically modified) is that there is more food being grown, with less waste and much fewer pesticides used. For poor countries, where some people can only afford rice to eat, the vitamin rice is helpful.

The bad side of GM food is that people have no idea what kind of consequences the genetic engineering of plants may have in the long run. Critics of GM food have nicknamed them "Frankenfoods" after the Frankenstein monster in the fictional story who was put together from spare parts! Will GM foods make it harder for small farms here to survive and for poorer countries to afford seeds? Will they change plants forever in unforeseeable and unnatural ways? Will they affect the people who eat them in ways we cannot yet predict?

All of these questions have led some countries to ban GM foods or put strong limits on them. Some people won't eat them at all. Only time will tell if GM foods are completely safe or whether they will be accepted by people as the next stage in food production.

38 FIND A BOOK ABOUT: RACHEL CARSON

Rachel Carson has been called "the mother of the modern environmental movement." She was an outdoorswoman who spent a lot of time exploring the forests of Pennsylvania and the rocky coast of Maine. She loved nature and the things she wrote about the environment have stirred people of several generations to value and protect the earth.

A biologist for the U.S. Fish and Wildlife Service, Rachel Carson believed that though humans are part of nature, they also have the power to hurt the natural environment. She worried about people using chemical pesticides and she wrote about it in her famous book called *Silent Spring*. The book warned people about the dangers of using pesticides and how it could affect the environment and human health. She testified in front of Congress in 1963, calling for new policies to protect the environment and people from the use of chemicals. This action and her book made such an impression on

President Kennedy (and others) that he ordered the testing of the chemicals of which she wrote.

Sadly, Rachel Carson developed breast cancer and died in 1964, but her life and books have encouraged people from many different backgrounds to protect the environment.

39 SHARE THIS ECO-STORY: JOHNNY APPLESEED

You have probably heard the name Johnny Appleseed, but you might not have known that he was a real person. His name was John Chapman and he lived in Massachusetts in the late 1700s. He made a name for himself by exploring the frontier wilderness, mostly in bare feet, and planting apple trees wherever he went. But he didn't just plant seeds. He would find a good spot in the wilderness, clear the brush, plant seeds and build a fence to protect them from animals. Some of his orchards covered many acres. When settlers moved into the area to start farms, they were very happy to see apple orchards already established and producing fruit. Many orchards in western New York, Pennsylvania, Ohio, Michigan, Indiana, and Illinois are thought to have been started by John Chapman's seeds. Some think he planted millions of seeds in his years in the wilderness.

40 KEEP A FOOD JOURNAL

Being responsible for your own diet is important. You want to make smart choices about what you eat, both for your own good and the good of your environment. Buy a journal and keep track of what you eat, and what you learn about what you eat.

Review what you write and see if you are eating and drinking as healthy as you can. If you write down what you eat and drink, you may become more aware that you need to drink more water, perhaps, or eat fruits and vegetables every day. You are the only animal on Earth that can pick up a pencil and paper and keep a food journal! So why not do it!

Be creative. Maybe as you create and plan your food journal, you can take steps to make your diet more interesting. Make notes to make sure that you try at least one new food a week, for example, or try a flavor of juice you've never had before. The more you try, the more you may find you like!

41 USE ONE GLASS!

When you get a drink of water or juice, do you fill up a glass, drink, then put the glass in the dishwasher—only to get a new glass later when you want something more to drink? You're creating more dishes to wash, which uses up water. Conserve! Choose a glass at the start of the day, and use it all day. Rinse it out, if you have juice, and if you drink water, you don't need to rinse it! You have many ways to conserve, even with the utensils you use every day.

CHAPTER 2

EARTH 101

42 VIEW THE EARTH FROM SPACE

When astronauts brought back the first color pictures of Earth from space, it changed the way mankind viewed its world. It was the first time that people could see the planet as the beautiful and fragile place it was. That picture stirred people to help preserve the earth and its amazing beauty in a way that nothing else ever had. Since that time, there has been an ongoing struggle to preserve our planet's natural beauty and clean resources while still having enough food, energy, and land for our more than 6 billion people to live.

43 GET MY DRIFT?

Millions of years ago our continents were not shaped the way they are today. As a matter of fact, they were not separate continents at all! Scientists now believe that the earth's land masses were once all one giant land mass called Pangaea. Over the last 250 million years, the continents have broken up and drifted to where they are today. Scientists call this Continental Drift. If you look at all the continents on a map, you can pick out how they all once fit together. Try it! Copy a map and cut out all the continents. Now try and piece them together looking at a map of Pangaea as a guide. Can you recreate the first supercontinent?

44 WORD UP!: CONTINENTAL DRIFT THEORY

Continental Drift is the theory that the continents drift apart and are still in motion today. Continental drift is one of the most interesting things that our wonderful Earth does. Why not share this term with your friends and look it up for some more information, together?

45 LEARN THIS ECO-TERM: PLATE TECTONICS

Plate tectonics describes the plate structure of the earth's crust and how they move.

46 MEMORIZE THIS: PANGAEA

Pangaea was the supercontinent that was made up of all the Earth's continents before they drifted apart 250 million years ago.

47 KNOW THIS: FAULT

A fault is where two of Earth's plates slide past each other. This is an area where earthquakes can occur.

48 WORD UP!: LITHOSPHERE

The lithosphere includes the outer part of the earth—the crust and the mantle, the 1,800 miles worth of rocky shell that can be found just below the crust.

49 CREATE YOUR OWN VOLCANIC ERUPTION

There are more than 500 active volcanoes in the world and most of them are found where two plates come together. Volcanic eruptions are most dangerous because of the toxic gases they release. Volcanic eruptions are thought to be responsible for putting about 110 million tons of carbon dioxide into the atmosphere every year—all resulting from some drifting plates!

For this activity, you will need one old mayonnaise jar, some baking soda, liquid dish soap, ketchup (optional), vinegar, and a sandy pile in your yard (optional). The carbon dioxide that is released when you mix the baking soda and vinegar is like a volcanic gas eruption!

1. Place the jar in the sink, or in a lasagna pan that can collect the "lava flow." You can bury the jar in a volcano-shaped pile of sand in your yard if you want to make this look like a real volcanic eruption. Maybe try it in the sink first as a trial run.
2. Add ⅛ of a cup of baking soda to the jar.
3. Squirt in some liquid soap.
4. Pour in ⅛ cup of vinegar (you can mix ketchup in with the vinegar before you add it, if you want to make the lava flow look red).
5. Stand back and watch your volcanic eruption!

50 MEMORIZE THIS: AQUIFER

Aquifers are places underground where water flows through sand, gravel, or even clay. People drill wells hoping to hit aquifers, which act as water sources for humans.

51 WORD UP!: PRECIPITATION

Precipitation is when water falls from the sky in the form of rain, snow, hail, sleet, or freezing rain.

52 LEARN THIS ECO-TERM: GROUNDWATER

Groundwater is the water that flows underground, filling soil and flowing out into springs and aquifers.

53 PLANTS AND THE WATER CYCLE

Do this exercise to learn about water cycles. You will need a plastic bag, a twist tie, and a tree or bush in your yard.

1. Take a gallon-sized plastic bag and cover a small branch—leaves and all—with it.
2. Close it tightly with the twist tie.
3. Come back the next day and look at it. There should be water in the bag with the twig. This is the water the plant lost in transpiration. Normally it would have evaporated into the water cycle.

54 KNOW THIS: END-PLEISTOCENE

The End-Pleistocene was a prehistoric time some 15,000 years ago at the end of the geologic time period called the Pleistocene. Many animals became extinct during this period.

55 WORD UP!: EPIPELAGIC ZONE

The epipelagic zone is the uppermost layer of the ocean, where phytoplankton—tiny plant-like structures that you can't see with the naked eye—get sunlight for photosynthesis (converting light into food).

56 GET TO KNOW: GLOBAL WARMING

Global warming is a term used to describe an increase in Earth's temperature from, in part, humans releasing large amounts of carbon dioxide into the air. Scientists believe that this will lead to climate change (a warmer Earth) that will have many bad effects on living things on the planet, including us! Some changes scientists expect include altered rainfall patterns, melting glaciers, rising sea levels, and numerous other impacts on animals and plants.

57 DO RESEARCH ON: RAINFORESTS

There are rainforests all around the world. Though a rainforest in South America may be home to many different types of animals and plants than a rainforest in Africa, what they all have in common is: high temperature, humidity, rain, and very tall trees. Rainforests get at least eighty inches (200 cm) of rain per year and have an average temperature of about 80°F (26°C). Rainforest trees are so tall because they are competing for the sunlight they need in a forest thick with vegetation. All this heat, moisture, and humidity make a very fertile environment. Scientists believe that rainforests may contain more than half of all the earth's species of animals and plants. This variation in life forms is called biodiversity. The rainforest is famous for its biodiversity because it has so many different species. Many of them haven't even been discovered yet!

58 CHECK THIS OUT: RAINFORESTS

Rainforests are very valuable to our global environment because their dense greenery collects more sunlight than any other habitat in the world. There is a lot of photosynthesis going on in the rainforest and that is a big part of the oxygen cycle, the process by which the world creates the air we breathe. Think of all those trees taking in carbon dioxide and releasing the oxygen we need. Rainforests are like giant, green filters for our atmosphere.

59 MAKE A RAIN SHOWER!

Rainforests are hot and steamy. When that warm, steamy air rises and hits the cooler air above, it rains! You can make your own tropical rain shower. You will need two pie pans, ice cubes, an oven mitt, cold water, an electric (plug-in) teapot, and help from a grownup.

1. Fill the teapot with water and plug it in. Place an empty pie pan on the countertop in front of its spout.
2. Add cold water and ice cubes to the other pie pan.
3. Put on your oven mitt to protect your hand. When the teapot boils, hold the pie pan full of ice water up over the steam rising out of the teapot spout.
4. The water vapor will begin to collect on the bottom of the ice chilled pie pan. It will cool and condense. Soon water droplets will begin to drip down into the bottom pie pan.
5. You have just created a rain shower!

60 SHAKE THIS ECO-FACT: RAINFOREST PLANTS

Many houseplants found in American homes were originally found in the rainforest: philodendrons, orchids, and bromeliads. Rainforest plants are adapted to survive in the dim sunlight under the thick forest canopy. That's a perfect trait for a plant that will live in your living room and only get a little light.

61 LEARN THIS ECO-TERM: SATELLITE

Satellites are objects that orbit around another object, like a planet. We use orbiting satellites for many technologies on Earth, including monitoring the weather.

62 MEMORIZE THIS: METEOR

A meteor is a rock or other matter that enters our atmosphere from space. Its burning passage toward Earth is called a shooting star.

63 WORD UP!: CLIMATE CHANGE

Climate change is a term used by scientists to describe a real change from one climatic type to another, for example from grassland to desert.

64 KNOW THIS: CONDENSATION

Condensation is when water vapor cools and changes back into its liquid form.

65 UNDERSTAND: ATMOSPHERE

We are surrounded by air, a gas layer held to the earth by gravity. The earth's gravity holds the air in an envelope around the planet that's about 6.5 miles (11 km) thick. This is called our atmosphere. The atmosphere is very important to protect us from things in space. The moon is covered with craters from being bombarded by meteors because it has no atmosphere to protect it. Most meteors that might hit the earth burn up in the atmosphere before reaching us. We perceive the streak of light as meteors burn up as shooting stars.

The atmosphere also protects us from the fierce ultraviolet light from the sun. It absorbs much of this light and lets just enough through to warm and nourish us. The atmosphere keeps us from getting too hot when our side of the planet faces the sun on a summer day or too cold when we are facing away from the sun on a winter night. It may sound like the atmosphere knows just what we need, but in truth, life on Earth evolved the way it did because our atmosphere provided the exact conditions we needed to live.

66 CUT THE ATMOSPHERIC LAYER CAKE

The earth's atmosphere is divided into five layers. The layers closest to the earth are the thickest and then get thinner and fade into space. A rocket leaving our atmosphere would have to go through each layer to get to space. When a rocket launches from Earth, it travels through the first layer, the troposphere. It is in this level of the atmosphere that all our weather occurs. This is where clouds form, as well as lightening, high winds, hurricanes, tornadoes, snow, hail, and freezing rain. It's a busy, bumpy place!

Next a rocket passes through the stratosphere where the air is calmer. This is where airplanes travel because the air is much less bouncy at this altitude. It is also where ultraviolet radiation from the sun reacts with oxygen to form ozone gas and the ozone layer. The ozone layer protects us from too much harmful radiation from the sun.

Next, the rocket flies through the mesosphere, the layer of the atmosphere that stops most meteors as they fly toward Earth. Then the rocket reaches the thermosphere. This is the layer in which a space shuttle would orbit the earth. A rocket could then pass through the exosphere, the outermost boundary of our atmosphere. This is where satellites orbit. From here a rocket leaves Earth's atmosphere and begins its journey into space.

67 WORD UP!: WEATHER

Weather takes into account the temperature, moisture, wind, and clouds and is what is going on in the atmosphere at any one time. One way to start talking to people about environmental issues such as global warming or pollution is to start a conversation about the weather. People like to talk about the weather. Older people, especially, can tell you stories about memorable weather they have experienced, like hurricanes or floods or even earthquakes. Enjoy these stories and ask questions. But also introduce topics about things that affect the weather, such as acid rain which you can learn more about in tip #118.

Talking about the weather is a great way to talk to people, discuss the environment, and learn something new at the same time!

68 MAKE YOUR VERY OWN CLOUD

You will need an empty, clear, two-liter soda bottle (no label) and its cap, warm water from the tap, a match, and help from a grownup.

1. Add about an inch of very warm water out of the tap into the bottle and lay the bottle on its side.
2. Squeeze the bottle (not enough to eject water), while your grownup helper lights the match, lets it burn, and blows it out near the opening of the bottle.
3. Release the bottle and it will draw smoke inside. This gives the water vapor something to condense around to form a cloud.

4. Screw on the cap and gently roll the bottle so the water coats all the sides.

5. Hold the bottle up to a bright window or lamp. See the smoky cloud? Now squeeze the bottle. This increases the air pressure and the cloud disappears.

6. Release the pressure on the bottle and watch the cloud appear again. By releasing the pressure on the bottle you have lowered the air pressure, simulating low air pressure up in the atmosphere where clouds form.

69 LEARN THIS ECO-TERM: SLASH AND BURN

Slash and burn is how some people clear forests for farming. It is when all the trees are cut down and then every thing remaining on the ground is set on fire to burn away. Slash and burn is a process that humans have used for millennia to clear land for agriculture or cattle grazing, but many people are turning away from this practice because it robs soil of its nutrients.

70 CHECK THIS OUT: RAINFOREST CLEARING

It is estimated that more than 35 million acres of rainforest are being cleared every year.

71 MEMORIZE THIS: ECOTOURISM

Ecotourism is when people visit a place to see the exotic wildlife and natural habitats. Many countries use money from ecotourism to help their economy while protecting their natural habitats.

If your parents are planning your next family vacation, offer to research some eco-friendly vacations you could take! Your parents may like the fact that you express an interest in your vacation and are willing to help plan it.

No matter where you go, remember that there are eco-friendly things you can do there to help the environment. For example, if you are traveling somewhere sunny and hot with water to swim in, you can buy eco-friendly sunscreen or eco-friendly protective swimsuits and outerwear.

Instead of going on a vacation where there are video games and amusement park rides, maybe you could go on a "nature vacation" and go camping or hiking. Wherever you travel, you always have lots of opportunities to learn about the natural environment. The more involved in the vacation you become, the more memorable and fun it will be for everyone!

72 WORD UP!: OASIS

Oases (plural of the word oasis) are places in the desert where water rises to ground level. It is in these spots that plants can grow and travelers can get water to drink.

73 LEARN ABOUT: DESERTS

The word desert often brings to mind endless miles of scorching sand dunes, but in truth deserts vary both in landscape and temperature. The Sahara desert, the largest hot desert in the world, is a sizzling belt of sand dunes that stretches the whole width of Africa. It can reach more than 125°F (51°C) during the day, with powerful winds sweeping across it. At night, with no plant life to hold the heat, the Sahara can drop to below freezing. Not all of the Sahara desert is made up of sandy dunes. Its landscape can vary from gravely flats to mountains, and dotted here and there are precious oases, which hold the only water and most plant life found in the Sahara. Oases have allowed some people and animals to make their home in the desert.

Another example is the Sonoran Desert, which has large, sandy plains and bleak mountains. It stretches over parts of southern California, Arizona, and northwestern Mexico. Branches of the

Colorado River run through it, so many trees, cacti, and shrubs find enough water to grow there. In Arizona, the giant saguaro and barrel cacti can be seen growing all over the desert. Beautiful flowering cacti and yucca make the desert seem more like a garden than the open sandy place one might imagine. When deserts do get rain, plants bloom and create seeds quickly to take advantage of the short-lived water supply. Heavy rains can cause flash floods and a dry riverbed can be a gushing river in just a few minutes. The desert is a habitat of extremes!

74 KNOW THIS: MIRAGE

A mirage looks like water in the distance but is actually shimmering light above a superheated desert plain. You may have seen a mirage on a hot day, on the highway. Have you ever been sitting in the car, looking ahead while one of your parents has been driving, and the road ahead looks a little darker than normal and fuzzy? That's a mirage!

75 DO RESEARCH ON: ENDANGERED DESERT SPECIES

Many of the animals on the endangered species list live in the desert. Some include:

- Desert tortoise
- San Esteban Island chuckwalla
- Desert monitor
- Desert bandicoot
- Bactrian camel
- Fresno kangaroo rat
- Arabian oryx
- Sonoran pronghorn

76 SHARE THIS ECO-FACT: BEATING THE HEAT

To live in a desert, plants and animals have to adapt to survive. Many animals are nocturnal and only become active at night when the air is cooler. Some animals go into a type of hibernation and sleep through periods of drought or extreme heat. This is called estivation. Some animals like the fennec fox develop large ears to cool off their bodies. The way this works is that the blood circulating through the ears is very close to the surface and is cooled by chilly nighttime desert temperatures. Some other desert animals can survive without drinking any water at all, but get all the moisture they need from the dry plants they eat.

77 LEARN THIS ECO-TERM: ERG

An erg is a big expanse of shifting sand in the Sahara desert. Go online and search for images of ergs—they can be very beautiful! You might have never seen a desert, in real life, but with the power of the Internet, you can look up all sorts of things. Use it to your advantage!

78 WORD UP!: ICE PACK

Ice pack is the thick mass of ice that covers Antarctica, Greenland, and much of the Arctic in winter. Ice pack is *not* the cold thing your mom puts on your knee when you bump it! Okay, well, it's that *too*.

79 GET TO KNOW: ANTARCTICA

Antarctica is the coldest place on Earth, sometimes reaching −130°F. It is one of our seven continents and includes the South Pole. The coast of Antarctica is windy and snow-covered, yet inland the Antarctic is a desert! The dry Antarctic interior is not like a hot sand desert at all, though it is considered the driest place on Earth. It is actually covered by a sheet of ice a mile or more thick, but there is rarely snowfall. It is a frozen desert. The Antarctic ice sheets may hold about 90 percent of all the earth's fresh water! Penguins, fur seals, leopard seals, Weddell seals, elephant seals, albatross, petrels, blue whales, killer whales, and krill all make their homes on or in the southern ocean around this frozen continent.

80 UNDERSTAND: ICEBERGS

Icebergs are huge chunks of ice that float in the ocean. They form in the warmer months when they "calf" off a glacier or ice pack. Most icebergs come from the edges of the Antarctic or Greenland ice sheets, so they are made of fresh water. They are usually a lot bigger than they look. The saying that something is "the tip of the iceberg" means that you are just seeing a little bit above the water. Usually only about one-eighth of the iceberg is showing above the water. Most of the iceberg is hidden underwater out of sight. This can be a hazard to passing ships. Interestingly, it is the smaller icebergs, called growlers, that can be the most dangerous because they don't show up on a ship's radar and can't be seen easily from above water.

81 MEMORIZE THIS: GLACIER

A glacier is a huge mass of ice made from compacted snow that moves very slowly. Glaciers are found in mountainous areas or near the earth's frozen poles. Did you ever see the 1997 movie *Titanic*? There was a glacier in that movie! I bet you can think of other times that you have learned about glaciers, too. Did you know that parts of the United States were even created by melting glaciers? Look it up to learn more! You might be living where a glacier used to be . . . you never know.

82 DRINK A POLAR TREAT!

Fill up an ice cube tray with blue raspberry juice (light blue colored). Then add three gummy bears to each ice cube spot. Let them freeze for several hours. Invite friends over and pop a couple of ice cubes into a little glass bowl for each person with a spoon. Polar bear freeze treats for all! Not only are ice trays reusable kitchen utensils, but you're remembering that the polar bears' habitat is in danger (from melting!) and we all need to keep the ice caps cold while you're eating them! To learn more about this, check out tip #129.

83 CHECK THIS OUT: THE ARCTIC

The Arctic isn't a continent itself, but includes the northern edges of Europe, Asia, North America, and Greenland and, of course, the North Pole. This is probably due to the fact that the Arctic is mostly frozen ocean—nine-feet thick frozen ocean! The only land included in the Arctic is called the arctic tundra, a treeless, frozen land covered in permafrost that only grows in the twenty-four-hour sun of the short Arctic summer. This boggy plain is a difficult place to travel, especially when fierce mosquitoes descend to feed on the animals living there. Musk ox, caribou, lemming, arctic fox, hare, wolf, and polar bear all contend with the fierce biting insects of the Arctic.

84 SHARE THIS ECO-FACT: FROZEN DESERTS

The largest desert on Earth is not a hot desert at all, but a freezing ice shelf—the interior of Antarctica. Though covered with ice, Antarctica rarely sees snow. Most of the snow falls on the coasts. This frozen desert, oddly enough, keeps much of the earth's fresh water locked in a thick sheet of ice more than a mile thick. Another cold desert is the barren, rocky plain between southern Mongolia and northern China called the Gobi desert.

The world's deserts are spreading, a process called desertification. A dry grassland is just a few days without rain away from becoming a desert. When overgrazed by livestock, desert plants, whose roots act to stabilize the soil and hold in the moisture, are lost. The topsoil dries up and can be blown or washed away. The grassland becomes a desert.

85 KNOW THIS: HIBERNATION

Hibernation is the period in which an animal spends the cold months of winter in a deep sleep. Different animals spend different lengths of time in hibernation. Do some research: you may be surprised at how long some animals stay in bed!

86 WORD UP!: ESTIVATION

As you read in tip #78, estivation is when an animal goes into a deep sleep through a very hot time. Can you think of any animals that do this? Why don't you look it up on the Internet or at the library? It's kind of like the opposite of hibernation—do you know what that is? Check out #85, for more information!

87 CHECK THIS OUT: GRASSLANDS

Grasslands are some of the most fertile lands on Earth. Much of our planet's grasslands have been plowed as farmland because the soil found there is so good for growing grains and other crops. That is why these areas have been named the breadbasket of the world.

These lands are also good for cattle and horses to feed in great herds. So much grassland has been plowed over that people have begun to worry that these lands will disappear completely. Some short and tallgrass prairies are now protected from development in small prairie preserves across the American Midwest. Africa has made national parks to try to protect disappearing wildlife that were being grazed over by domestic livestock. In the future, we will have to find a balance between keeping some natural grasslands for the wildlife and using others for growing the food we need.

88 SHARE THIS ECO-FACT: PRAIRIE FIRES

Prairie fires are an important way for grasslands to renew themselves. Some plants need fire to make their seeds sprout. The burned grass acts as a fertilizer for the next plants coming up. Large animals can outrun the flames, but smaller animals escape fire (and predators) by seeking safety in burrows underground. Here they are safe from raging prairie fires that sweep across the plains.

89 DO RESEARCH ON: TYPES OF WETLANDS

Though all wetlands have water in common, there are many different kinds of wetlands in the world. There are marshes, often found on the edges of ponds and lakes. Marshes are open wetlands dotted with reeds, sedges, and grasses such as cattails. Swamps, on the other hand, are often thick with shrubs and even trees. Walking through a swamp can be hard and even dangerous. Mangrove swamps form along coastlines where rivers meet the sea. The water there is brackish, which means that it is a little salty, but not as salty as the ocean. Mangroves are important for protecting shorelines from storm flooding and erosion.

Bogs form from shallow ponds that have slowly collected plants and leaves until they are thick with them and other plants like moss and ferns root right over the water in the rotting plant matter. Over time this makes a thick mat on top of the water that is called peat. Like plastic wrap over a bowl, no air can get in and the rotting plants beneath build up acids. As a result, animals and plants that fall into bogs rot very, very slowly. These are just a few of the many kinds of wetlands in the world.

90 CHECK THIS OUT: WETLANDS

Wetlands have so much water that the soil can actually be washed free of its nutrients. Plants have to be adapted to a water habitat to survive there. A few kinds of plants have adapted and get extra nutrients by trapping and absorbing insects! Pitcher plants, sundews, and Venus flytraps all are insectivorous plants found in wetlands. Each plant has its own amazing adaptation for trapping insect prey.

91 TEACH YOURSELF ABOUT: ENDANGERED WETLAND SPECIES

Many of the animals on the endangered species list live in wetlands, including:

- Bog turtle
- Aquatic box turtle
- Spotted pond turtle
- California tiger salamander
- Alaotra grebe
- Hawaiian common moorhen
- Atlantic, Chinook, Coho, sockeye, and chum salmon
- Catfish
- Sturgeon
- Steelhead trout

92 GET TO KNOW: OCEANS

When you look at a map of the world, you can see many different oceans, but in fact they are all connected, covering three-fourths of the earth. The Pacific is the largest ocean, followed by the Atlantic, Indian, Southern, and Arctic Oceans. Oceans are so vast and huge that they have many different kinds of habitats in them. The surface of the ocean, where sunlight can reach, is called the epipelagic zone. It is where most sea life is found. Here millions upon millions of tiny phytoplankton float along, making their living on the energy of the sun using photosynthesis. They are at the bottom of the food chain in the ocean and many animals feed on them. In this layer of the ocean we find most of the fish, sharks, rays, jellyfish, marine mammals, and sea turtles.

The ocean and seashore can be a very fragile and sensitive ecosystem. When we think of a beach, the first things we think about are sand, water, and other people, but the next time you are at the beach, notice all the other natural life around you. There are birds in the air, insects in the sand, and in addition to fish in the ocean, there are mollusks and crabs and even sea creatures you cannot see! Some large beaches have information centers where you can learn about the animals and organisms in the seaside environment. Be sure to respect the beach and the ocean, because this is where all those animals and organisms live. It's their home, and you're just a visitor!

93 DO RESEARCH ON: ENDANGERED AQUATIC SPECIES

Many of the animals on the endangered species list live in the oceans, including:

- Green sea turtle
- Hawksbill sea turtle
- Leatherback turtle
- Loggerhead sea turtle
- Hawaiian monk seal
- Stellar sea lion
- Bowhead whale
- Gray whale
- Humpback whale
- Sperm whale
- Finback whale
- Blue whale

94 CONSIDER THE SAFETY OF CORAL REEFS

Coral reefs are one of our most biologically diverse habitats, but they are also very delicate and are in serious danger. In 1998, President Clinton helped establish the U.S. Coral Reef Task Force to better preserve and protect coral reef ecosystems. Here are some ways you can help preserve and protect coral reefs:

95 SPREAD THE CORAL REEF WORD!

Coral reefs are always under pressure from collectors, who harvest the colorful corals and fish for aquariums and other markets. Snorkeling tourists sometimes walk on the fragile plants and animals, and boaters pollute the delicately balanced habitat.

96 CORAL AND BOATING—LESSONS TO SHARE

There are some basic rules you and your family should remember when it comes to boating near or on a coral reef. First of all, never run your boat into coral! You can usually spot coral—just watch for their brown color in shallow water. Also, don't ever anchor a boat on coral. Use a coral reef buoy, if there is one, or anchor in the sand nearby.

97 BE CAREFUL AROUND CORAL—IT'S IMPORTANT!

Before you participate in normal boating activities, think about the coral around you. Never dump trash or dirty water (bilge) near a coral reef. They are sensitive! Also, don't troll (drag a hook) near a coral reef. Hooks can injure coral.

98 PROTECT THE CORAL'S BEAUTY

We all know that coral can be beautiful—just take a look at images on the Internet, if you haven't seen any coral up close in real life. It's natural to want to snorkel or swim near coral, in order to get a better look, but make sure you never step on it! Think of it this way: Coral is a living animal—how would you like to get stepped on?

99 DON'T HELP THE HARVESTERS!

Don't support coral reef harvesters. Never buy coral for your fish tank unless it has been stamped with the Marine Aquarium Council (MAC) stamp. This makes sure the coral was raised for aquariums and not from a wild reef.

100 UNDERSTAND: THE PARTNERSHIP BETWEEN ALGAE AND CORAL

Coral reefs have a partnership with algae called zooxanthellae. Zooxanthellae algae live in the coral tissue itself. They help the coral by providing food and oxygen while taking up the carbon dioxide the coral releases. For algae, it is a safe place to live and grow. Zooxanthellae algae are what give coral its many pretty colors. They are very sensitive. If the coral reef becomes polluted or if the water temperature changes, zooxanthellae algae will die and the coral loses its pretty colors. This is called coral bleaching and is a sign of an unhealthy coral reef.

101 LEARN THIS ECO-TERM: BENTHIC ZONE

Humans rarely get a chance to see the ocean habitat on the bottom of the ocean, known as the benthic zone. Animals here have to be able to live in total darkness and survive under extreme water pressure. Some have adapted some strange survival traits, such as glowing in the dark!

If you live near an aquarium, pay a visit with your family and seek out any exhibits they may have about organisms or aquatic life that live in the benthic zone. If you don't live near an aquarium, tell your parents that you'd like them to plan your next family vacation near one!

102 LEARN ABOUT: TIDE POOLS

Tide pools are another distinct ocean habitat. They are found where the oceans meet the shorelines. The low tide zone has the most species of any of the ocean habitats since it gets ample sun, water, and is protected from pounding waves. Animals in tidal zones have to adapt to wave action by developing anchors so they won't get washed away, plus they must be able to move to stay wet in the changing tide. That's a lot of adapting!

103 DO RESEARCH ON: KEYSTONE SPECIES

People don't always understand the interconnections in an ecosystem. If an animal is considered a pest, we often try to get rid of it. Sometimes getting rid of a single link in a web can upset the whole ecosystem and make things a lot worse. This is especially true if the animal is a keystone species. A keystone species is one that is so interconnected with the other species in its ecosystem that its disappearance changes the balance of the whole ecosystem. An example of this would be bees: To some people, bees are pests. But they help pollinate flowers and help plants grow, making them crucial to much of the food production in the world.

104 SPREAD THE WORD ABOUT: THE SEA OTTER

One example of people altering an entire ecosystem involves a little mammal on the California coast—the sea otter. Fur traders hunted the sea otter almost to extinction in the 1700 and 1800s. But then fishermen began to see changes in the ecosystem with fewer sea otters. Sea otters are one of the few animals that eat sea urchins. When the otters disappeared, the sea urchin population grew rapidly. Sea urchins, in turn, feed on kelp. The kelp beds are important to several fish populations as a place to spawn, or create new generations of fish. So with the otters gone and the sea urchins on the rise, the kelp beds began to disappear too. Then the fish, having lost their spawning site, disappeared as well. Suddenly, in just a few years, the fishermen found that the fish were gone.

Then, in 1911, the United States, Great Britain, Russia, and Japan passed a treaty that protected sea otters from hunting (the North Pacific International Fur Seal Treaty). In the areas where sea otter numbers recovered, the sea urchin populations were brought back under control. The kelp beds recovered, and the fish population came back, too. This is an example of how the destruction of one keystone species can affect a whole ecosystem.

105 GET TO KNOW: WILDWAYS

Many conservation groups have formed to try to protect and restore "wildways." These are wild areas from Canada to Mexico that are linked together to provide migration paths for birds and mammals. This is important to try to reduce the fragmentation of wild areas and the effect that has on wildlife. Migrating birds and mammals need safe wild areas to rest, feed, and travel through in the changing seasons.

106 MEMORIZE THIS: SEMI-ARID

Semi-arid is a word that describes habitats that are very dry, but which are not considered deserts. Semi-arid land areas are home to scrubby plants and hardy animals. Can you think of any semi-arid places that you've traveled to? Ask your parents for help figuring this out. You can look at a globe or a map to see where you might have visited one!

107 UNDERSTAND: DESERTIFICATION

Sometimes the difference between a desert and a dry grassland is just a few inches of rain per year. The grasses hold the soil in place and the habitat, though dry, is relatively stable. With desertification all of this changes. There are many reasons why grasslands turn into desert, and the one you might think is the most obvious—a long drought—is actually rarely the reason, although it does happen!

It is almost always due to the actions of humans that desertification changes a habitat.

In the 1930s the great plains of the United States experienced desertification from overgrazing, poor farming practices, and drought. It was called the "Dust Bowl" for the dust storms that swept soil across the Midwest and lasted for ten years, causing huge hardship to many people.

One big reason for desertification is overgrazing. A semi-arid grassland that is overgrazed by cattle loses the little protection it has. With no plant roots left to hold it in place, topsoil blows away in the wind or washes away in the next rain. The land becomes a desert. Twenty-four billion tons of topsoil are lost every year to erosion by wind, water, and other causes.

Another way desertification happens is when a forest is completely cleared by slash and burn technique, which you can read more about in tip #69!

This is when all the trees are cut down and then everything is set on fire to burn it away. The thin topsoil that is left exposed to the elements has nothing to hold it in place, and just like overgrazed land, the soil blows away in the wind or washes away in the next rain.

A river valley can turn into a desert when people reroute water from the river upstream for irrigation or to supply a city with drinking water.

108 DO A DESERTIFICATION EXPERIMENT

Desertification is usually caused by poor agricultural practices compounded by drought. You can test this theory with a simple experiment. You will need: a potted plant, another pot of soil about the same size as the plant (it should never have had a plant in it, just soil), a fan, some old newspapers, a sunny spot by a window, and some time.

1. Set the two pots side by side in the window. Water them both the same amount. Then let them sit for a week with no water.
2. After one week (depending upon how sunny it is) they both should be pretty dry. Now you can water the plant, but NOT the soil. The plant represents how areas with vegetation have more active water cycle activities going on, so the planted habitat will

get some rain. The empty pot represents the overgrazed terrain that is getting no rain activity.

3. After about a month of watering the plant once a week (and not watering the drought stricken overgrazed region) you are ready to demonstrate the consequences of desertification.

4. Lay both pots on newspaper next to a wall. Make sure the newspaper comes up the side of the wall a bit to protect it.

5. Now turn on the fan facing the plants against the wall. Let the air blow on both pots. It can be light breeze or a strong gusty wind.

6. What effect did the wind have on the two pots? Did the plant and moist soil protect the potted plant from losing as much soil as the empty, dry pot? This is a simplified look at the extreme consequences of desertification.

109 SHARE THIS ECO-STORY: THE ARAL SEA

One extreme case of desertification occurred in Russia, where farmers tried to divert the waters that fed into the Aral Sea to irrigate their crops. Over time, the Sea began to shrink. As it shrank, the water got saltier. Soon, it was too salty for the fish to live in it. The Sea was dead. Where it dried up, it left a flat, salt desert. Now when the wind blows, the salty sand blows out into the hills and ruins surrounding farm fields. In some places, giant ships sit stranded out in the sand as if they were dropped from space. This is one extreme result of manmade desertification. People are now trying to take measures to stop desertification throughout the world. Limiting grazing animals in dry areas and planting trees or building sand fences to block winds helps to slow the process, but it will be a constant challenge to keep the desert from creeping into our drier lands.

110 RECYCLE FOR TREES!

Start a bottle drive to raise money to buy trees to plant on your school grounds. Make up a flier to put up around school and town about it. This has two advantages. You get to recycle bottles and cans and you get to plant new trees!

111 PLANT A TREE

Planting trees is a fun way to act green and to help the environment. All trees, as you now know, make oxygen and take away carbon dioxide. They also hold the soil with their roots, add shade, shelter for wildlife, cool the air temperature, lower noise pollution, and block wind. They are worth adding to your neighborhood!

112 PICK GOOD TREES TO PLANT

The best time to plant trees is in the spring when it is still cool. Then the tree has all summer to grow and take root. There are a few ways you can find good trees to plant. You can ask your parents to call your county cooperative extension, soil and water conservation district, or you could just call a local nursery. If you want to order a bunch of little trees, you usually have to do this by March so that the trees will arrive in April. Trees that start out the size of your finger are called "seedlings." You can plant them in paper cups on your windowsill for a couple of weeks if you aren't ready to plant them outside. Seedlings are a good way to plant a lot of trees. Not all of them will survive, so it's good to plant more than one at a time. You can order trees that are a little bigger too—these are called "transplants." They may have a better chance at survival, but are a little more expensive to buy. Some types of trees are easier to grow than others. Evergreens, like white pines, do very well being moved or "transplanted" and grow fast. You should know what kinds of trees do well in your area before you order them. The safest thing to do is to consult someone at your local nursery.

113 TAME WILD TREES

When your parents and you do yard work, you probably focus on the plants, flowers, and grass. But don't forget about the trees on your property! Big trees and little trees are often neglected in the midst of other tasks, but you shouldn't assume that all trees can stand alone (get it?). Trees need watering sometimes, pruning, and even just cleaning. You can help the trees in your yard live long and strong by learning how to clear dead branches from the base, strip away diseased bark, water it when needed, and watch out for its well-being—especially during storms and other weather events that might damage the tree.

114 GET STARTED PLANTING TREES

You may want to just dive into the whole tree-planting process, but before you do, make sure you do some research! Unfortunately, planting and growing trees might take a bit more work than you imagine. Before you go to the nursery, check out the web and look at what trees will thrive in your neighborhood. Also, when you have your parents take you to the nursery, make sure to talk to the people working there about what you will need to do and how to give your new tree its best shot! Every set of seeds is different and every tree will be a unique, growing gift. Won't it be cool to watch something grow from nothing? If you do it right, it could be in your yard for years and years to come!

115 START A TREE-PLANTING CLUB!

Order ten trees for each person in the club. They can each plant their trees somewhere in their yard, schoolyard, or neighborhood (always ask your principal at school or neighbors before planting trees on or near their property). If you have ten members, that's 100 trees you've added to the world!

116 MAKE YOUR OWN PLANT GUIDE

Be the only one in your neighborhood who knows all the names of the trees on the block. Make your own guide. You'll need a few sheets of white paper, a soft-tipped pencil or charcoal, a heavy book, a three-ringed binder (an old recycled one will do), a hole puncher, and a tree guide from the library.

1. Collect one leaf from each tree in your yard. If it is an evergreen collect a small stem with a few needles or bundles of needles on them.

2. Place them between two pieces of paper and press them flat under a heavy book overnight.

3. Take your newly flattened leaves out and lay each under a piece of paper and do a rubbing with a soft-tipped pencil by shading in the entire area surrounding where the leaf lies under the paper. Take away the leaf and then use the pencil to darken the outlined leaf drawing and its features. (You might be able to fit three or four leaves on each 8.5" x 11" sheet of paper.)

4. Using a tree guide, identify your tree types and write their common and Latin names under each leaf. Punch holes in each sheet to fit your binder and collect them inside.

5. When you discover new trees, add them to your collection!

CHAPTER 3

FIGHT POLLUTION!

117 SAVE YOUR BREATH: AIR POLLUTION

Though you may not notice it, the air around you holds many things besides the mixture of gases you breathe. It holds water vapor, dust, pollen, and sometimes—pollutants. Pollutants are things that are in our environment that may be harmful to us. Where do pollutants come from? Air pollution can be smoke from a forest fire or chemicals released from a factory smokestack. It is the exhaust from our cars, trucks, boats, buses, planes, and even lawnmowers! It can also be chemicals straight from your home such as paint, varnish, or turpentine fumes. Chemical pesticides sprayed on crops pollute the air, as do methane gases from rotting garbage in landfills.

Air pollution can affect your health. It can also affect the health of crops, forests, and animals. It can even damage the protective ozone layer in our atmosphere. Air pollution can make a haze in the sky so thick that you cannot see the mountains.

Not all pollution is manmade. Sometimes natural events can cause air pollution, like a volcano erupting, natural gas (like radon) escaping into the air, or a lightning strike setting off a forest fire. Even dust blown off dry land can be considered air pollution. All of these things are natural parts of our environment, but can still create air pollution that can harm us.

118 DO RESEARCH ON: ACID RAIN

Acid rain affects the northeastern part of the United States more than any other. Some lakes in the Adirondack Mountains in upstate New York have become so acidic that fish and frog populations have begun to disappear. Acid rain even causes buildings and statues to corrode over time. Why is acid rain so bad in this area? There are three main reasons. One reason is the weather. The main winds in the United States blow from west to east. The second reason is where the pollution is made. Smokestacks in the industrial cities of the Great Lakes region of the United States and Canada belch out a lot of pollutants, which are easily carried by the winds to the northeast. The third reason involves people. To try to decrease local air pollution, the factory owners made their smokestacks taller. This pushed the pollution higher up in the atmosphere and blew it eastward with the strong winds. While this made the local people much happier, it blew the pollutants right into the northeastern states.

119 DON'T LOWER YOUR pH

Acidity is measured on a pH scale. Something with a pH of 1 is the most acid and something with a pH of 14 the most base (or alkaline). Pure water is considered to be neutral (it has a pH of 7). Normal rainwater has a pH of about 6. That is a little acidic. That is because even pure rainwater falls through carbon dioxide in the air. Rain with a pH of less than about 5.3 is considered acid rain. Rain in the northeastern states has a pH between 4 and 5. This is seriously acidic rain.

120 SEE ACID RAIN'S EFFECTS ON LAKES AND FORESTS

Rain might seem like the cleanest source of water on Earth—after all, the only place it has been is in the clouds. However, rain and snow are affected by what they pass through on their way to the ground. Some factories release nitrogen and sulfur from their smokestacks. This mixes with clouds to create falling rainwater containing weak nitric and sulfuric acids. Then the rain (or snow) carries the acid to the ground, into lakes, streams, and forests. It changes the pH making the soil and water more acidic than they would be naturally. Acid rain can make the soil too acidic for some plants to grow and can slow the growth of trees. In lakes and streams, it can make the water environment too acidic for fish, frog, and salamander eggs to hatch. If lakes and ponds become acidic enough they will eventually become completely lifeless.

121 DO AN ACID RAIN EXPERIMENT

How does acid rain affect plants? Try this experiment to see.

1. Plant three bean seeds in three separate pots, place them in the window and let them grow. When all three plants are about four inches high they are ready to be tested.
2. Label the plants 1 to 3.
3. Always water #1 with one cup of fresh water.
4. Always water #2 with one cup of fresh water mixed with 1 teaspoon of vinegar.
5. Always water #3 with one cup of fresh water mixed with 2 tablespoons of vinegar.
6. After a week can you see a difference in how the plants look? How about after two weeks? Write down the effects of the weak acid and strong acid treatments.

7. This is what acid rain does to plants. It weakens them, and in some cases, can kill them.

Over decades acid rain can actually corrode buildings and statues. Try this experiment to see how this happens.

1. Fill one glass bowl with water.
2. Fill one glass bowl with vinegar.
3. Add a piece of chalk (the same size) to each bowl and leave them over night. Chalk is made from a similar mineral that some buildings are made of: limestone.
4. In the morning take out both chalk pieces. Are they still the same size?
5. Over a long period of time acid rain corrodes buildings the way the vinegar corroded the chalk.

122 TEACH YOURSELF ABOUT: THE GREENHOUSE EFFECT

Our atmosphere keeps the earth's temperature stable. It lets just the right amount of sunlight through to keep the earth from getting too hot in the summer. It also keeps warmth from escaping so we don't get too cold in the winter. In this way, the atmosphere acts like a greenhouse. This is called the "greenhouse effect." It is part of what makes our planet a comfortable place to live.

123 SAVE THE OZONE

Ozone in the atmosphere protects the earth from the sun's powerful ultraviolet radiation. This blanket of protection is called the ozone layer. Over the last twenty-five years, something has been breaking down the protective ozone layer. Scientists discovered that chemical compounds called CFCs (chlorofluorocarbons), which are in aerosol sprays and refrigerants (coolants), were actually destroying the ozone faster than it could be replaced. Check out tip #312 for more information on coolants.

124 WORD UP!: OZONE-DEPLETING GASES

Ozone-depleting gases are CFCs, refrigerants (coolants), aerosols, solvents, methyl bromide fumigant, and halon fire extinguishers. (Don't forget, you'll learn more about coolants later!)

125 GET TO KNOW: GREENHOUSE GAS

Scientists have been worried that too many "greenhouse gases" are building up in our atmosphere. Humans are driving more cars and heating more homes than ever before. We do this mostly by burning fossil fuels (oil and gasoline) and coal. This burning releases greenhouse gases, like carbon dioxide, into the atmosphere. At the same time we are cutting down trees in record numbers. Trees, as we have learned, help take up carbon dioxide in the atmosphere and replace it with the oxygen we need. Scientists worry that if we have fewer trees and make more carbon dioxide, we will begin to build up greenhouse gases faster than ever before. This might block even more heat from escaping into space. Like a greenhouse with its windows shut on a hot, sunny day, the Earth will warm up. Greenhouse gases include water vapor, carbon dioxide, methane, nitrous oxide, and ozone.

126 KNOW THIS: METHANE

Methane is a flammable gas that is made when organic matter decomposes. It is a greenhouse gas.

127 DO A GREENHOUSE EFFECT EXPERIMENT

How would the greenhouse effect warm up Earth's climate? Try this experiment to see. You will need two jars, two inexpensive, metal cased thermometers, two dark washcloths, a paper and pencil to record results, one lid, and a sunny window.

1. Put a dark washcloth inside each jar. Lay the jars on their side in the sunny window.

2. Lay one thermometer inside each jar facing up so you can read it.

3. Put a lid on one jar. Leave the other one open.

4. Watch the thermometers closely for twenty minutes. Check the temperatures every two minutes and record the time and temperatures.

5. After twenty minutes, open the jars and remove the thermometers.

6. What difference did you notice in the temperatures between the two jars?

7. Explain what you see.

128 DO RESEARCH ON: GLOBAL WARMING

Global warming is a term used to describe an increase in the earth's temperature from, in part, humans releasing more carbon dioxide into the air. Scientists believe that will lead to climate change, which will in turn have many negative effects to living things on the planet.

129 SHARE THIS ECO-FACT: SATELLITES

NASA studies Earth from space via satellites. From here they can see changes in the shape and size of the polar ice caps. They can see that the year-round ice pack in the Arctic is shrinking. Over the past twenty-five years, the polar ice cap has shrunk by 10 percent. Scientists have also been watching satellites that have been collecting the earth's surface temperatures for twenty years. They show that the temperatures are rising. In 2003, the largest ice shelf in the Arctic—one that had been in place for 3,000 years—broke up into the ocean. Climate does change naturally over time, but rapid changes are unusual. These facts may signal global warming.

How will melting ice caps affect the planet? For one thing, the bright white ice caps reflect a lot of the sun's energy back to space. As the ice caps shrink, more sunlight will be absorbed by the earth, warming the climate even more. Melting ice caps would make more water available for the water cycle, which could change the rain patterns and alter how salty the ocean is around the poles, affecting fish populations.

The shrinking ice shelf is already affecting arctic animal populations. Species like polar bear, that hunt seals off ice shelves, are unable to find prey as easily without the frozen platforms.

Scientists have found that hungry polar bears are drowning while trying to find prey on their usual hunting grounds.

130 MELT SOME "ICE CAPS"

Will the melting ice caps dilute the ocean's salt water around them? Will that raise the ocean levels? To test this you will need two clear glasses, some ice, and a dark liquid.

1. Fill both glasses half way with a dark liquid, like grape juice or cola.
2. Then fill the rest of one glass with ice.
3. Leave them both on the counter until all the ice is melted.
4. Look at both glasses. What do you notice? The glass with the melted ice is fuller, the water level rose. The dark liquid is also lighter, meaning it has been diluted. If that liquid had been salt water like the ocean, it would be less salty now!

131 FIGHT OCEAN POLLUTION!

Ocean pollution can come in many forms. It can result from oil tankers spilling oil, boats sinking, or even people littering. Large or small, ocean debris can cause problems for both sea life and humans. Garbage gets into the ocean when people dump it off boats and litter beaches, but it also can reach the ocean from rivers, storm drains, or ocean dumping of industrial waste. Eventually all water on land flows toward the sea.

Besides being ugly to look at, a lot of ocean debris, like plastic bottles, bags, Styrofoam peanuts, old fishing wire, and nets, is quite dangerous to wildlife. Whales and dolphins eat plastic bags thinking they are squid; sea turtles and ocean birds eat Styrofoam peanuts that block their digestive tracts; and abandoned fishing nets tangle and drown thousands of seals every year. Even human swimmers and divers can get tangled in dumped nets and drown.

Other dangerous ocean pollutants include human sewage, oil spilled at sea, and medical waste dumped in the ocean. These hazards endanger both ocean animals and human swimmers and wash up on our beaches. Fish and shellfish become so toxic from absorbing pollutants that they are not safe for people to catch and eat either. This affects lobstermen and fishermen's livelihoods.

132 CLEAN UP YOUR OWN OIL SPILL

How hard is it to clean up an oil spill at sea? Try this simple activity to see. You will need some dark-colored olive oil, a pie or cake pan, a feather, some of your dog's fur (brush it off, don't cut it off!), some dishwashing soap, and a spoon.

1. Fill a cake pan half full with water. Drip in some olive oil. You have created an oil spill!

2. What happens to animals that swim through an oil spill at sea or walk through an oil spill on the beach? Drag the feather and then the dog fur through the oil. What happens? It sticks. Can you imagine how hard it would be to clean off thousands of birds and mammals?

3. Shake the cake pan gently to create wave action. See how the oil breaks up and spreads around. It still doesn't mix with the water, but it spreads. This is why oil cleanup in the ocean has to happen fast.

4. Try to scrape the oil out of the water with a spoon. It's very hard to get it all, isn't it?

5. Try using some other cleanup materials like paper towels, cotton, or a square of cloth. How do these work?

6. Now add more oil in the center of the pan again till you have a little pool (about a tablespoon). Drip a couple of drops of dishwashing soap right into the center of the oil. What happens? What happens when you shake the pan gently? Isn't it surprising how well the soap dissolves the oil? Soap is a strong solvent. So why don't they just dump lots of liquid soap on oil spills? Would you want soap in your drinking water? How would soap affect all the sea animals? Would it be even worse than oil? Aren't you glad you didn't have a real oil spill to deal with?

133 LEARN THIS ECO-TERM: ECOLOGICAL FOOTPRINT

An ecological footprint is the amount that each of us affects the earth by using its resources.

Don't worry though, you shouldn't be anxious about using some of the earth's resources—all living things use some resources just by being alive. We breathe in the earth's air, drink the earth's water, and eat the earth's food. We cannot help but have an ecological footprint. The important thing is not to be wasteful, and to do what we can to make our ecological footprint as small as possible.

134 MEASURE YOUR ECOLOGICAL FOOTPRINT

Being aware of how your actions affect the planet is the first step in conservation and becoming "green." Our "ecological footprint" measures how much land and water it takes for each of us to survive. How big a footprint you leave depends upon how much of the planet's resources you use up. Do you know how many resources you use up? Think about the resources in your environment that are natural and manmade, and note which ones you use. Then, of the resources you use, estimate how much you use in a day, a week, or a year. Take water, for example: How much water do you drink every day? How much water is in the soda or juices you drink? How much water do you use to bathe, water plants, or for play? Talk with your friends or parents about how you could measure (and reduce) your use of resources.

135 UNDERSTAND: LIGHT POLLUTION

Light pollution is a problem in many cities throughout the world. It comes from streetlights, building lights, outdoor lights, and advertising lights for stores and other businesses. From a distance you can see the glow of many cities in the night sky. Some cities give off so much light that they can be seen from space!

136 WORD UP!: SKY GLOW

Sky glow is the light glow in the night sky over cities. It makes viewing the night sky difficult.

Depending on where you live, the sky glow may be slight or it may be significant. In some very large cities such as New York City, you may only see a few of the brightest stars in the sky because there are so many lit-up buildings in the city. But if you travel to a state like South Dakota or Montana or Arizona and go where there are almost no buildings, you may look up at the night sky and be amazed at how many stars you see! Many tourists visit these states from the large cities where they live and say: "I didn't know there were so many stars in the sky!!"

137 DO A LIGHT EXPERIMENT

You can easily test how light pollution affects what you can see in the night sky. On a clear night, lie out in your backyard. Make sure all your outside lights are off and any inside lights that shine into the backyard. Let your eyes adjust until the night sky is clear. Look at all the stars and the details you can see. Now have someone turn on the outside light. Look at the stars now. Are they as clear as they were before? This is light pollution!

You can help prevent light pollution and save energy by turning off lights when you aren't using them, by using lower watt bulbs if you don't need bright lights, and by only using lamps where you absolutely need them.

138 SEE THE DANGER OF TOO MUCH LIGHT!

Too much light can waste energy, but it also has an effect on people. Light, like sound, crosses boundaries and can frustrate neighbors, shining into their homes and keeping them awake at night. Glaring lights can blind drivers and cause accidents. Bright lights in the workplace all day long can lead to headaches, high blood pressure, and nervousness.

Too much light can make seeing stars harder. Astronomers and people who want to look at the stars must go to an area with fewer lights to get a better look. Observatories are located in low light areas and get regulations to keep the areas that way. For example, when the California Institute of Technology built their Observatory on Palomar Mountain in the 1930s, they chose that spot because it was so dark that the 200-inch telescope could see very faint, distant galaxies.

But over the years southern California has become very built up and the lights of its cities have caused "sky glow" in the night sky. The Palomar Observatory has tried to work with local governments to keep the light down so they can continue their important astronomy work.

139 REALIZE THAT NOISE IS POLLUTION, TOO!

Noise pollution doesn't just hurt a person's hearing, though over time it can lead to permanent hearing loss. Noise can also add to stress, raise blood pressure, and can even contribute to heart disease! Noise can anger and frustrate people when they are awakened from sleep or when it makes it difficult for them to concentrate. Noise near schools can affect children's ability to pay attention in class, learn new things, and concentrate on reading. Noise pollution can even frighten wildlife and interfere with important behaviors such as eating, mating, and migration.

140 I SAID: "SUPPORT NOISE BARRIERS!"

Many towns and cities have noise rules and regulations and many things are being done to reduce the racket out there. Highway departments put up noise barriers between big highways and neighborhoods. These can be grassy hills, trees and other vegetation, or sometimes just a big, cement wall.

141 DO A NOISE POLLUTION EXPERIMENT

Can noise pollution keep you from learning? With a group of friends try this experiment. You will need two rooms, a pair of earplugs, and two copies of a short poem (four lines or fewer).

1. Choose two people as learners. They each get a copy of the poem to learn.
2. Put one person in a room with the door closed and earplugs in their ears. They have five minutes to learn the poem by heart.
3. The other person sits on the floor of the second room while you and a couple of friends talk and make noise around them. They have to try and memorize the same poem in five minutes as well. They cannot cover their ears.
4. At the end of five minutes bring both learners into one room. Have the learner who dealt with the noise try to recite the poem out loud from memory first. Then have the silent learner try. Who

remembered more of the poem? What does this tell us about noise pollution and learning?

142 REDUCE NOISE POLLUTION

You might not think about noise as being pollution, but like air and water pollution, noise pollution can cause illness in humans and wildlife. Most loud noise throughout the world comes from types of transportation: cars, trains, and planes. Other sources of noise include machines, power tools, office equipment, garden and lawn equipment, and even music. By lowering noise pollution, you're helping your environment.

143 LESS PACKAGE IN YOUR PURCHASE

Buy products with less packaging. The less we throw away, the less debris is around in general.

If you buy a product such as a toy or a game and you think there is too much wasteful packaging, you can write to the company that made the product and ask that they use less packaging in the future. If they cannot use less packaging, perhaps they can explore more eco-friendly alternatives, or make it easier for people to recycle the packaging.

144 SNIP RINGS

Cut the rings of six-pack can holders in case they make their way into the ocean. Birds and aquatic wildlife think those rings are food, and they can get caught in the plastic and even die.

Even when you are in your home and you throw away one of these plastic rings, it is a good idea to snip it before you throw it into the trash. You never know if your trash bag, as it travels from the garbage truck to the landfill or wherever it goes, will break open and a bird will find that plastic ring. It's also possible that your trash bag could travel on a barge on the water and break open, making the ring accessible to aquatic life.

So snip before you toss!

145 STAMP OUT LITTERBUGS

Talk to your friends about not littering . . . ever! And if you see some trash in a park or on the beach, carry a bag with you and pick it up.

146 KEEP BEACHES CLEAN

Volunteer to help clean up your local beach. Get your friends to help, too. When you're done, you can swim as a reward to yourselves!

147 WATCH FOR GAS SPILLS

On March 24, 1989, the Exxon Valdez, a huge oil tanker, hit a reef off of Prince William Sound in Alaska. The hull of the ship cracked open and spilled more than 11 million gallons of crude oil into the Sound. That oil spill was the largest in U.S. history. A spill that large is catastrophic anywhere, but a spill in Prince William Sound was even harder to deal with because there was so much wildlife to save and clean up. Afterward, Congress passed the Oil Pollution Act of 1990. It created stricter rules for oil tankers, their owners, and captains. According to the new requirements, tankers have to have stronger hulls and ship captains have to be in better contact with vessel traffic centers. No one wants a spill like that to happen ever again.

It is worth noting, however, that more gas is spilled every year when people fill up their lawnmowers, weed trimmers, and chippers than was spilled in the entire Exxon Valdez oil spill. Remind your parents to be careful when filling up machinery with gasoline.

148 DON'T LET PLASTIC BAGS BLOW AWAY

Plastic bags that are lost in the wind travel a long way. Sometimes they can blow out into the ocean, where they may hurt ocean animals.

Sea turtles sometimes eat plastic bags, thinking they are jellyfish. This can block their stomach and cause them to starve. Seals, whales, and dolphins can also be hurt the same way. Plastic bags also get pushed in the wind against fences, building up into an ugly mess. They clog drains, sewers, and intake fans. They have caused such a problem in some countries that they have been banned, and people who still use them are taxed or fined. More recently, some American cities, such as San Francisco have banned plastic shopping bags because of the hazards they pose and because it takes hundreds of years for them to biodegrade.

149 DISPOSE OF TOXIC STUFF SAFELY

Never, ever pour antifreeze, oil, or other chemicals on the ground, into storm sewers, or down the drain. Find out where your local waste disposal facility is and let your parents know. Also find out when the next toxic waste day is in your town landfill and talk to your parents about getting rid of old paint cans and other yucky stuff in your basement and garage. Throwing out toxic waste properly makes the world a safer place and your home should be the safest place on Earth!

150 DO YOU KNOW ABOUT "NATURAL" POLLUTION?

It's hard to believe, but not all pollution is manmade. Sometimes natural events can cause air pollution, like a volcano erupting, natural gas—like radon—escaping into the air, or a lightning strike setting off a forest fire. Even dust blown off dry land can be an air pollution hazard. All these things are natural to our environment but still make air pollution that can harm us.

151 TAKE ACTION WITH TRASH AROUND YOUR NEIGHBORHOOD

Take the time to pick up trash. It's worth it to keep your environment clean, and it's easy to do. Just store a garbage bag and gloves in your parent's car so you can pick up the trash you see around your neighborhood.

152 GET YOUR FRIENDS INVOLVED IN TRASH PICKUP

Organize a "trash pickup" hike in your neighborhood. Take turns hiking through each of your friend's neighborhoods. This can be a really fun weekend activity—it can bring you closer to your friends, you get to spend time outside, and you're helping the environment, too!

153 YOU CAN ADOPT A HIGHWAY, TOO!

Have you ever seen those signs on the highway that say "This highway was adopted by" or "This highway is clean with thanks to . . . ?" If you can raise the right amount of help by talking to the adults around you, you too can adopt a highway! Enlist the help of your family, class, or club—and get ready for regular litter pickups there.

154 COMBINE AWARENESS AND ACTIVITIES

As with neighborhood trash pickups, you can have fun while being active and spreading awareness, too. Why not have a picnic in the park or on the beach and pick up litter in the area afterward? Maybe the other people in the park or on the beach will see you doing this and change their ways too!

155 MAKE A LITTER STICK

Pick up trash without bending down or having to touch dirty litter by making a litter stick. Use an old wooden broom handle, a tree branch that the wind knocked down, or buy an inexpensive paint roller stick from the hardware store. Ask a grownup to hammer a headless nail or a long finishing nail (with no head) into the end of the stick. You have a litter stick. Now go stab some litter!

156 ORGANIZE A LITTER CLEANUP HIKE

Get some friends together and look at a map of your town. Plan where you will hike: in a park, maybe. Make the first hike about a mile long to see how long it takes. Make sure everyone wears clothes that are right for the weather and comfortable shoes. Have everyone bring work gloves and a trash bag. As you walk around town, take turns picking up the litter you see on the street. One person can carry a recycling bag to hold the recyclable bottles and cans you find.

157 MEMORIZE THIS: SMOG

Smog is ground level ozone and particulate matter formed by burning fuels on hot, sunny days. The word smog came from the combination of the words *smoke* and *fog.* Have you ever seen smog? If you live in or close to a city, you most likely have!

158 MAKE SOME SMOG

Create you own smog in a jar. All you need is one jar, an aluminum foil top, some ice cubes, some paper, matches, and an adult to help. Everything has to be done fast so be sure to have all the materials ready.

1. Rinse the jar out, so the sides are coated with water.
2. Form a lid with the foil and set it aside with the ice cubes on top to cool.
3. Have your adult helper light the paper and drop it into the jar. Quickly put on the cold foil lid with the ice cubes on top.
4. See how the smoke sits on the bottom of the jar? This is the way smog forms.
5. Don't breathe it in when you release your smog outside. It's bad for you!

CHAPTER 4

ANIMALS

159 SHARE THIS ECO-FACT: FISHERMEN

It is hard to make fishermen stop fishing when fishing is the job they have always done. It also may be one of the few good jobs on an island or in a coastal village—people have to feed their families. Plus no one owns the ocean. Anyone in the world can move around on the ocean and fish where they please. For these reasons, it is not easy to get people to stop fishing long enough to let fish populations recover.

160 CHECK THIS OUT: FISHERIES

Many countries have begun to grow their own ocean fish in saltwater fisheries. This may help relieve the pressure on the depleted ocean fisheries. But to really save our ocean fisheries, people will have to fish only at rates that would give fish populations time to recover.

161 TRY DIFFERENT FISH

The U.S. Fisheries Department keeps track of fishing levels in the oceans. The fish that people most like to eat (and thus, the fish fishermen most like to catch) are cod, haddock, and blue-finned tuna. These are the fish that have become the most endangered from overfishing. The U.S. Fisheries Department rates populations of fish from abundant to depleted. All three of these most popular fish plus many others are rated as depleted.

162 KNOW THIS: EXTINCT

A species becomes extinct when the last one of its kind dies. Can you think of any animals that are extinct? There is one—very famous—group, that hasn't been around for years . . . you're right! It's the dinosaurs. But we know they were around millions of years ago because we have found evidence in the fossils they left behind.

Fossils are impressions of organisms that lived a long time ago that have been preserved in the rocks. The fossil record shows us when species became extinct over the passage of millions of years.

Many museums have fossils on display—why not ask your parents to take you some time?

163 WORD UP!: ENDANGERED

A species is considered endangered if there are so few of them that they may soon become extinct. Can you think of any endangered animals? Bet you can! Think really hard. Sadly, there are lots of them. And if you want to learn more, research how those animals that you come up with actually became endangered.

164 LEARN ABOUT: ENDANGERED SPECIES ACT

Passed in 1973, the Endangered Species Act is meant to protect threatened and endangered plants and animals from going extinct. It also is meant to protect the habitats where endangered species are found. As studies show how the populations of plants and animals are doing, the numbers of plants and animals on the list changes. If an animal like the bald eagle recovers, it is taken off the endangered animal list and moved to a threatened animal list. If an animal like the bactrian camel becomes so scarce that it is threatened with extinction, it is added to the endangered animal list.

165 LEARN WHY THINGS BECOME ENDANGERED

Most species become endangered because of loss of habitat. If an animal has no place to live, it will go extinct. So the Endangered Species Act gave the U.S. Fish and Wildlife Service (FWS) and the National Oceanic and Atmospheric Administration Fisheries (NOAA) the job of picking habitats in specific locations on land or in U.S. coastal waters that needed special protection to house endangered species.

Did you know that when the American alligator became endangered from overhunting, all the fish started to disappear? That was because alligators eat a large fish called a gar, which feeds on many kinds of game fish. When the alligators disappeared, the gar populations exploded and they ate all the fish! Not until the alligator was protected and began to recover did the gar populations come under control, allowing the fish to come back too.

There are about 1,880 species listed under the Endangered Species Act. As many as 1,310 of them are found in United States and its coastal waters. The rest are found in other countries. Some of our most endangered species on Earth include:

- White rhinoceros
- Black-footed ferret
- Yangtze dolphin
- Ibex
- Sumatran rhino
- California condor
- Snow leopard
- Giant panda
- Mountain gorilla
- Orangutan

To see the full list, go to: *www.fws.gov/endangered/wildlife .html#Species*.

166 SPREAD THE WORD ABOUT: THE PEREGRINE FALCON

The peregrine falcon was once very close to extinction because of the use of the pesticide DDT. The chemical was sprayed in wetlands to kill mosquitoes but moved up through the food chain as birds ate the insects and falcons ate the birds. DDT didn't kill the falcons outright but caused their eggs to have soft shells and break, so no new young could be born. Once scientists discovered what DDT did in the food chain, the chemical was banned, and slowly, animal populations began to recover. With a lot of help from wildlife biologists and a captive breeding program, peregrine falcon numbers have recovered. Now it is not unusual to see these amazing predators nesting on skyscrapers in New York City, or hunting pigeons!

167 LEARN THIS ECO-TERM: THREATENED

When species are not quite endangered but their numbers are low, they are considered threatened. You can find lists of the threatened animals on the Internet. Since we are aware of animals that are at risk and can educate ourselves on what's happening to their species, maybe we can save them!

168 DO RESEARCH ON: THE DODO

Dodos (DOH-DOHZ) were flightless birds that lived on isolated islands off the coast of Africa. When sailors finally found the islands in the 1600s, it took only eighty years for the dodo to become completely extinct.

169 SHARE THIS ECO-STORY: EXTINCTION

It is true that people have—through overhunting, development, habitat destruction, and careless introduction of predators—caused countless animals to go extinct. There are many examples of this to look at.

Big mammals have often been hunted to "protect" people and their livestock. That is exactly what happened to the Caspian tiger, which became extinct in the late 1950s. This tiger, which lived on a swath of land that stretched across the Middle East, around the south end of the Caspian Sea and into Asia, was driven to extinction by the Russian army. Russian soldiers were ordered to kill all the tigers to open up the region to development such as factories, towns, and roads. Once the tigers were gone, towns established themselves and the whole region became more developed and less "wild," making the area inhospitable to tigers.

Even if overhunting is the main cause of an extinction of an animal, habitat loss is usually part of the story. Fewer than 200 years ago, there were grizzly bears that roamed out on the American prairie. The plains grizzly was a fearsome sight to early settlers. Yet even these giant animals lost their habitat to the droves of new settlers invading the West and soon disappeared. Now plains grizzlies can only be found in some wild prairies in Northern Canada, where few people live to disturb them.

Many species balance on the edge of extinction from habitat loss and may not last another generation. These include some of our favorite animals, like the panda, orangutan, tiger, snow leopard, and mountain gorillas.

170 MEMORIZE THIS: POACHING

Poaching means to hunt fish or animals illegally: that is, to hunt animals that are endangered, or to trespass onto private land to hunt, or to hunt where it is not allowed.

It can be very sad to read stories or to do research into poaching, because sometimes the animals that are poached are very beautiful: the hunters want their beautiful skin or some other part of them. Remember that the best cure for being sad is to learn something, because then you have the power to do something about the problem!

171 GET THE TRUTH ON POACHING

Poaching does not just happen in Africa or Asia. There is a lot of poaching in our own National Parks right here in the United States! People steal cacti, trees, tortoises, and even grass if they can sell it. It's a frustrating problem for those of us who want to protect our disappearing national treasures.

There are many ways you and your family can help stop poaching.

172 SAVE THE IVORY ANIMALS!

Never buy, sell, or own anything made from ivory. Even ivory that has been acquired legally drives the sale up of, and indirectly the poaching of, ivory. Remember, all ivory represents the death of an elephant or walrus.

173 KEEP UP THE CORAL CRUSADE

We talked about some of the dangers that coral reefs face . . . but did you know there are coral poachers, too? Whatever you do, don't support coral reef poachers. Never buy coral for your fish tank unless it has been stamped with the Marine Aquarium Council (MAC) stamp. This makes sure the coral was raised for aquariums and not taken from a wild reef.

174 PICK YOUR PETS CAREFULLY

Don't keep exotic animal pets, even if you see them at the pet store. The exotic animal pet trade, though legal if regulated in the United

States, is not regulated in all countries around the world. So owning exotic animals does drive the hunting of exotic species. It's best to leave wild animals in their natural habitat.

175 GET TO KNOW: ENDANGERED RAINFOREST ANIMALS

Rainforests are also valuable because of the vast array of animals, plants, and giant trees that live there. Rainforests all over the world are being cut for timber. When the trees are gone, all the animals, insects, and plants disappear too. The environment is completely altered. The humidity that clung to the trees evaporates away. Erosion washes the thin soil away. Rainforest land is often cleared and burned for farmland, even though the soil in these areas is thin and not very good for growing crops. It is estimated that more than 35 million acres of rainforest are being cleared every year. Since rainforests are so important for decreasing carbon dioxide and creating oxygen for the oxygen cycle, no one knows for sure what will happen when all the rainforests are gone.

Many of the animals on the endangered species list live in rainforests. They include:

- Aye-aye
- Chimpanzee

- Gibbon
- Jaguar
- Ocelot
- Mountain tapir
- Gorilla
- Lemur
- Orangutan
- Tiger

176 KNOW THIS: SPAWN

Spawn is another word for fish laying their eggs upstream. Can you think of a word similar to spawn? Maybe a word used to describe how other animals protect and harvest their eggs? It's interesting to compare how animals treat their young differently, across species.

177 BUILD A BUTTERFLY GARDEN

Butterflies feed on the flower nectar of certain plants. To attract butterflies, you can plant these plants in your garden, or you can grow flowers that their caterpillars like to eat. The butterflies will lay their eggs on those plants. Some examples of flowers that butterflies like are: cosmos, Queen Anne's lace, zinnia, butterfly weed, coneflowers, New England asters, spearmint, milkweed, yarrow, phlox, and daylilies. Plant these and you won't just have butterflies, you'll have a beautiful garden!

178 DO YOU KNOW YOUR YOUNG ANIMALS?

Baby animals are our Earth's future. When they grow up and find mates, they will keep their species alive. So do you know what a baby zebra is called? How about a baby whale? Check out the list below to bone up on your baby knowledge.

Adult	Young Animal	Adult	Young Animal
Bear	Cub	Beaver	Kitten
Caribou	Calf	Deer	Fawn
Duck	Duckling	Eagle	Eaglet
Eel	Elver	Elephant	Calf
Falcon	Eyas	Fish	Fry or Fingerling
Frog	Tadpole or Pollywog	Goat	Kid
Goose	Gosling	Insect	Nymph or Pupa
Kangaroo	Joey	Lion	Cub
Ostrich	Chick	Otter	Whelp
Rabbit	Bunny	Rhinoceros	Calf

Sea Lion	Pup	Shark	Cub
Sheep	Lamb	Swan	Cygnet
Tiger	Cub	Toad	Tadpole
Whale	Calf	Zebra	Foal

179 GROUPS OF ANIMALS

Now that you know your babies, can you remember what you call a big group of these animals? Test yourself here!

- Colony of ants
- Army of caterpillars
- Gang of elks
- Gaggle of geese
- Nest of hornets
- Leap of leopards
- Swarm of locusts
- Covey or bevy of quail
- Bale of turtles
- Pack of wolves

- Hive or swarm of bees
- Herd of elephants, caribou, or horses
- School of fish
- Horde of gnats
- Mob or troop of kangaroos
- Pride of lions
- Bed of oysters
- Knot of toads
- Nest of vipers

180 WORD UP!: NOCTURNAL

Nocturnal animals are active at night and rest during the day. I bet you can think of a couple of nocturnal animals. Some may even live in your neighborhood—you might hear them when you're lying in bed at night.

181 UNDERSTAND: ORDER

Scientific classification is a system by which we group and categorize organisms. Order is the classification level where animals are grouped between their class and family. The levels start with kingdom and then progress to phylum, class, order, family, genus, and species. For example, the wolf is in the animal kingdom, and is in the chordate phylum. Its class is mammal, its order is carnivore, its family is canine, its genus is Canis, and its species is lupus.

182 LEARN THIS ECO-TERM: INVASIVE SPECIES

A species that is introduced into an area where it does not normally exist will often alter the environment there. The lack of natural enemies in the new area often leads to outbreaks in population causing harm to native plants or animals.

Some invasive species have a worse effect than others. For example, sailors who brought dogs and pigs to a small group of protected islands off the coast of Africa led to the downfall of the flightless dodo, whose ground nests were plundered by these non-native predators.

Weasels and cats brought to New Zealand also devastated the ground-nesting and flightless birds living there. Goats introduced on the Galapagos Island have stripped vegetation, making it more difficult for other animals to live there. Many countries now have rules about bringing any plants or animals into their country. They have learned some hard and expensive lessons from past introductions of foreign species.

183 SPREAD THE WORD ABOUT: THE WATER HYACINTH

Since settlers first began coming to America, they have introduced hundreds of invasive species. These include: fire ants, the Asian long-horned beetle, Africanized honeybees, ladybugs, gypsy moths, starlings, and many more. It is a costly and difficult problem to get rid of invasive species once they get into an ecosystem.

In 1884, at an ornamental plant exposition in New Orleans, American gardeners got their first glimpse of the beautiful purple flowers of the water hyacinth, a native plant of South America. A Florida gardener took a cutting back home and dropped it into his garden pond. Within weeks the water hyacinth had taken over the pond. To get rid of it, he pitched it into the St. John's River. This began a century long battle to get this aggressive plant back under control. The water hyacinth grows at an amazing rate, spreading floating mats of vegetation so thick that it blocks light to the underwater environment, killing lakes and ponds. People tried to chop it up and then burn it, only to find that each small piece started a new plant! They brought in manatees to graze on the plants but the plants spread quickly up rivers and canals. Within a few years the water hyacinth had spread to several southern states. Finally, in the 1960s, people started spraying the water hyacinth with herbicides. Herbicide, a strong, toxic substance that poisons plants, did kill the water hyacinth, but it also meant that the poison got into rivers and lakes.

184 LEARN ABOUT: KUDZU

Kudzu, an invasive vine from Japan, was brought to the United States because it grew fast, was a good groundcover, and helped stop erosion. But as it grew over whole forests it began to block sunlight, causing all of the trees to die. It grew over barns, houses, fences, and power lines. Controlling kudzu has not been easy. The most effective control found so far is grazing goats!

185 MEMORIZE THIS: BIOLUMINESCENCE

Bioluminescence is when an animal such as a firefly or deep sea fish, gives off its own light. This can be a beautiful sight! Look it up online to see photos—you won't be sorry!

186 DO RESEARCH ON: FOSSILS

Fossils are impressions of organisms that lived a long time ago that have been preserved in the rocks. The fossil record shows us when species went extinct relative to the passage of millions of years.

187 ANIMALS CAN LOSE THEIR HOMES, TOO

There are many animals that are close to extinction from habitat loss. The giant panda, tiger, snow leopard, and mountain gorilla are among them. What can be done to save them from extinction?

188 HOW TO STAVE OFF HABITAT LOSS

In order to make sure that animals like the giant panda, tiger, snow leopard, and mountain gorilla don't go extinct, we have to make it a priority, as humans, to protect the habitats in which they live. There are many organizations and charities that help preserve wildlife habitats. Look one up today and join in the cause!

189 BE CAREFUL WITH WHAT YOU BUY

Many hunters and poachers break the law and kill these animals so they can profit from selling fur, tusks, or another rare commodity. When buying things, especially souvenirs while on vacation, make sure you think about where the product came from and if an animal was hurt in the process. If we stop buying these things, maybe the hunters will move on to a different business!

190 SPREAD YOUR NEW KNOWLEDGE!

Now that you know all about poachers and their products, make other people aware so they know not to buy products made from endangered animals and maybe we can save them after all!

191 SUPPORT NEW HABITATS

Animals need as much habitat as they can get to be successful. Usually all you hear about is people destroying habitat. You rarely hear about people making new animal habitats. The truth is that it doesn't happen very often and when it does, it is usually by accident. But what a great accident!

One unexpected kind of animal habitat that we have created is in landfills and garbage dumps. They may be gross, but they provide food and shelter for many mammals, birds, and insects. It is thought that the grizzly bears in Yellowstone Park would have gone extinct in the 1950–60s if it hadn't been for the garbage dumps there. The same goes for sewers and subway systems, cow barns, agricultural fields, and orchards. Many manmade places provide alternate habitats to adaptive animals.

On a more pleasant note, flower gardens create habitat for nectar-feeding animals like butterflies and hummingbirds. Vegetable gardens can house and feed slugs, snails, snakes, rabbits, and beetles. One thing is for sure—humans do affect habitats with our presence.

192 UNDERSTAND: HABITAT LOSS AROUND THE WORLD

Habitat loss is a very serious problem on our planet today. All animals have a habitat in which they live, whether it's a vast rainforest or a tiny anthill. They have food to eat and a safe place to sleep and raise their young. They compete for food with other species and protect their habitat by being territorial or migrating from place to place to find more food. When humans clear a forest for farming or to build homes, whatever animals live in that forest lose their habitat. This is a very serious threat to animals that have a limited habitat. It can lead to extinction.

As the human population expands, more and more natural habitats are destroyed to make way for the needs of humans. Fragmented habitats result, with some areas developed while others are left wild. The animals that survive may move into the smaller fragments of their habitat. This increases competition and stress in the remaining habitat. It can result in some species dying out. This decreases the biodiversity of the habitat, and thus, our planet.

193 DO RESEARCH ON: PANDAS AND HABITATS

One example of how habitat loss affects a species is the giant panda. Although protected from hunting and listed as an endangered species since 1984, panda numbers are still declining. This is because the giant panda feeds almost totally on bamboo, and the bamboo forests have been cut down to make way for the ever-expanding population in China. The pandas are left in small, isolated bamboo forests separated by development. Bamboo is a species that has an occasional die-off period, that is, it temporarily dies off as a result of natural causes. If this occurs in an isolated area where pandas live, they can't get to another bamboo forest to feed. Because of this the giant panda is one of the most endangered mammals in the world. It is believed that there are fewer than 1,600 left. There is so little nutrition in bamboo that they have to eat for fourteen hours a day to get calories and cannot even stop eating to hibernate without starving! Unless the Chinese can stop development of panda habitat, it is just a matter of time before the pandas will be lost forever.

194 SHARE THIS ECO-STORY: BATS

Another example of humans creating a habitat involves bat populations in upstate New York. In that region there are very few natural caves, so the one animal that needs a cave habitat to survive the winter—bats—were never very numerous in the state. Then in the late 1000s, people started mining for ore in New York's Adirondack Mountains. For many years, men dug miles and miles of underground mines and extracted ore. When the mining ended, they left miles of what were essentially caves. Over the last century, seven species of bats have established residency in these caves in upstate New York. All of them are small, insect-eating bats. The old mines act as perfect winter hibernation caves. The air temperature there stays at about fifty degrees all winter so the bats can sleep safely and emerge in the spring to hunt for insects. The Adirondacks can be very buggy in the spring. The advantage for the people near the bat caves is that these bats can eat up to 500 mosquitoes an hour!

195 FIND A BOOK ABOUT: JANE GOODALL

Primatologist Jane Goodall lived in the jungles of Africa for twenty-five years watching chimpanzees and recording observations about their lives. The things she saw taught us a lot about our closest animal relatives. Her observations changed how people thought about chimpanzees and permanently altered how we treat primates throughout the world. In 1977, she founded the Jane Goodall Institute to help save habitats, teach about the environment, and keep primate research and protection going in Africa (primates include chimpanzees and monkeys but also humans). To this day, Jane Goodall spends much of her time speaking around the world and sharing her message of hope for the future. She wants to encourage young people to make a difference in their world.

CHAPTER 5

PLANT LIFE

196 TEACH YOURSELF ABOUT: BIODIVERSITY

Biodiversity refers to how many different kinds of plants and animals there are in one place. The rainforest is famous for its biodiversity because it has so many different species, many of which have not even been identified yet.

Biodiversity is not just how much wildlife there is, but the different kinds of wildlife. Each different habitat, from rainforests to polar regions, has a variety of animals, plants, and fungi. Why is biodiversity so important? Every organism in an ecosystem plays some role in keeping things healthy and in balance. The overlapping jobs of organisms act as backup in case of drought, disease, flood, or fire. This complex tapestry of life has evolved over millions of years. Even the smallest microbe in the soil plays its part. When species begin to disappear from an ecosystem, the entire balance is altered.

197 SHARE THIS ECO-STORY: CORN

An example of the danger in losing species variety can be shown with modern corn. American farmers over many generations bred the best-tasting sweet corn and planted only that pure strain year after year. This is called a "monoculture." Then a fungus called "corn smut" attacked the crop. The corn had been bred to be so specific that it had little resistance to the fungus. Entire corn crops were destroyed. Agricultural researchers went to Mexico and searched out the wild maize that corn was descended from to find the gene that resisted smut and bred it back into the corn. Now farmers plant a variety of crops and strains to avoid the dangers that occur when crops lose their healthy biodiversity.

198 KNOW THIS: MONOCULTURE

Monoculture is when farmers plant one type of crop only, with no variety. Can you think of some examples of crops that might make up a farm's total produce? What about corn? Or have you ever seen one of those sunflower fields that seem to go on forever? If you had a farm, would you want to make one crop—and what would it be?—or would you want to have lots of different ones? What would you plant?

199 WORD UP!: BIOFUELS

Biofuels are fuels made from recently dead plants and animals. These fuels are usually used for transportation. Recently, car companies have started producing cars that use biofuels—a step representing a great advancement in technology. Keep your eyes peeled for the little logo on the back of many cars that says "hybrid" or "biofuel." When you spot one, you know that person is concerned about the environment, too—just like you!

200 SAVE WATER WITH CACTI

Cacti are easy houseplants to keep because you rarely have to water them. There are many cool kinds of cactus. It's fun to start a collection on your windowsill, just make sure you buy your cacti from a good plant store that only buys from certified nurseries and not from people who poach cactus from the desert.

As you will see when you visit your local nursery, cacti come in all shapes and sizes. If you talk to someone who works there and ask them about which cactus would be the best kind for you, you will end up learning more than you knew when you first walked in! The salespeople at the nursery are very knowledgeable and like to talk about plants, so go ahead and ask questions.

201 LEARN THIS ECO-TERM: BIOMASS

Biomass is the amount of any plant or animal matter that grows and can be used to make energy. Can you think of an example of biomass? It might help to look this one up or ask your teachers about it. Biomass is all around us—you just have to learn to be able to recognize it!

202 MEMORIZE THIS: BOTANIST

A botanist is someone who studies plants. Botanists may work in a nursery, teach at a college, or travel the world looking for new plant species. You might have a botanist in your own back yard! Does someone in your family read a lot of books about plants? Does he or she use the Internet to look at growth patterns and best conditions? Are you a botanist yourself? You just might be!

203 GO ON AN URBAN SAFARI

Though you don't often think of cities as having wild areas, green spaces in urban areas can be home to a multitude of animal and plant life. Even a patch of weeds in an abandoned lot can house insects like butterflies, moths, ants, bees, beetles, and even cockroaches. Wild mammals like mice, rats, raccoons, skunks, squirrels, falcons, ducks, and seagulls can also be common. Even reptiles and amphibians can be found in and near city park ponds. Take a pad and paper and go downtown to a city park. Sit on a bench and look around. What animals do you see? Birds? Squirrels? Write down everything you see. Take some time to really look and listen. Do you hear birds calling? Do you see insects of any kind around you? Bees? Butterflies? There are a lot more animals in urban habitats than you might have thought, right?

204 PLAN AN URBAN GARDEN

Urban gardens are a great way to provide food and habitat to urban wildlife. Try these small gardens. Take a fork and a packet of flower seeds called alyssum—they come in white or pink. Use the fork to loosen the soil between cracks in the sidewalk (a less-used sidewalk is better). Sprinkle the seeds in the loosened soil. Water them. Check on it later. They will bloom all summer!

205 USE THAT WINDOWSILL!

Place a pot of soil on your windowsill. Plant flower seeds that birds and butterflies will like: daisies, zinnias, bee balm, and fuchsias.

206 MAXIMIZE OUTDOOR SPACE!

Place any hardy potted plant out on your fire escape or front step. String it with berries, popcorn, or small seeds. Watch the birds come visit! Attract birds to a tree outside your window the same way.

207 SAVE A TREE

Try having a live Christmas tree this year. Instead of buying a cut tree, purchase a large potted evergreen. Or you can start the summer before and buy a balsam fir or blue spruce from a nursery and keep it in a large pot through the fall. Bring the tree inside before it gets too cold. Be sure and keep watering it all winter, since it won't be getting any rain indoors! Then dress it at Christmas time. It might be smaller than the trees you are used to having, but it will make the pile of presents look a LOT bigger. Then next summer, plant it in your yard!

208 KNOW THIS: DEFORESTATION

Deforestation, when trees are stripped from the forest, is a terrible thing that is happening in this world. Have you heard or read the phrase "Save the Rainforests?" What they are really talking about is the problem of deforestation. But it can happen everywhere—not just rainforests. It might be happening in your backyard. Have you seen a lot of trees cut down simply to build a new house or building on that property? That's deforestation!

209 GET TO KNOW: LIFE AFTER DEFORESTATION

The effects of deforestation are sometimes surprising. Yes, it's sad to see a beautiful rainforest cut down and to know that the animals have lost their habitat, but these are not the only reasons to worry about deforestation. Rainforests play a part in our global environment. They house many different kinds of animals and plants, helping to preserve biodiversity. They play a role in the oxygen cycle, supplying badly needed oxygen to our atmosphere, while taking in the carbon dioxide we make when we breathe out. They hold moisture in the atmosphere, acting like giant, green sponges. When you cut down a rainforest, you lose the protective cover of the trees and the bare ground is pounded by rain, losing its topsoil to erosion. Once gone, new soil can take generations to develop. Plus, what happens to the soil that gets washed away? It can cause other environmental problems. It washes downhill into rivers and builds up. This is called sedimentation. The river fills in and gets shallower. Boats then can't travel in the shallow waterways. The river can become murky, making fishing a lot harder. All of these things affect the lives of the people and animals in and around the rainforest. These are just some of the dramatic side effects of deforestation.

210 DO AN EROSION EXPERIMENT

When forests are completely cut down, much of the soil's protection is removed. Serious erosion can result. Try this experiment to see what happens to the soil that's left behind. You will need a patch of open soil outside—a garden spot before any seeds are planted is perfect—some grass clippings, some dead twigs, a hose with a spray nozzle, and a gardening trowel (little shovel).

1. Loosen the soil with the trowel, and make three mounds a few inches high.
2. Leave the first mound as it is. It is an area cleared of trees completely.
3. Cover the second mound with grass clippings and stick in a few (three to four) broken twigs. This is an area that has been cut for timber selectively.

4. The third pile should get twig trees stuck into it thickly like a forest, then top it with a blanket of lawn clippings in between. This represents an uncut forest.

5. Using the hose on the widest spray pattern (with the least water pressure), spray the three mounds evenly. Spray them until tiny streams of water are running down the unprotected mound. Turn off the water.

6. Examine the three mounds. How did they each fare under the hose's spray? Did the unprotected mound wash away with no vegetation to protect it? Did the timbered mound have less erosion than the unprotected mound? How did the forested mound do? Can you guess how a clear-cut forest would fare in a big rainstorm?

211 WORD UP!: IRRIGATION

Irrigation is when manmade water channels are used to bring in water to grow crops. Hoses and sprinkler systems help to irrigate the plants and grass in your backyard, but some farmers use irrigation techniques on a much larger scale—by building levies and damns and even advanced drainage systems.

212 LEARN THIS ECO-TERM: PEAT

Peat develops in wetlands from built up rotting vegetable matter. Ever heard of peat moss? Does someone use this peat moss to feed the plants in your family's garden? If you want to learn more about peat, why not head to your local nursery and talk to an employee for some more information?

213 RID PLANTS OF PESTS, THE GREEN WAY

Try spraying soapy water on your houseplants or garden vegetables if they get pests on them. It can work as well as chemical pesticides and it is not poisonous. Plants can attract all sorts of pests, including insects from outside. Soapy water is the clean, safe, green way to keep your plants and house clean!

214 MOW LOW

According to the EPA, Americans have covered 25 million acres of our country with lawns. That is roughly about the size of the state of Pennsylvania. Lawns use tons of water, are often treated with chemical fertilizers and weed killers, and need to be cut every few days. Lawnmowers, edgers, weedwackers, and hedge trimmers all are expensive and need gallons and gallons of gas to run. They are also noisy! Lawns replace natural habitats of native plants that are used by birds, butterflies, and other animals. Ask your parents if you could plant some native bushes. These bushes are good cover for birds and other animals, reduce the amount of grass to mow, and can be very pretty!

215 MEMORIZE THIS: PERMAFROST

Permafrost is the layer of soil just below the surface, mostly in the polar regions of the earth, that stays frozen year round.

216 DO RESEARCH ON: GREEDY GRASS

According to the EPA, every lawn that is just 100 feet wide by 100 feet long needs 10,000 gallons of water each year to stay green. The most popular grass planted in America for lawns is Kentucky bluegrass, because it is soft, thick, and green. The only problem is that it needs thirty-five to forty inches of rain every year to stay green, even though most places average only about fourteen inches or fewer. This means a lot of clean drinking water is pumped onto these lawns to keep them green. What a waste! Even worse, people who want the perfect lawn often add fertilizer. Homeowners in America put 67 million pounds of chemicals on their lawns every year to this end. That's more pounds of fertilizer than farmers use!

Ask your parents to let part of your lawn grow wild with wildflowers and native grasses. They can even put a fence around it like a garden. It's a great way to attract birds and butterflies.

217 KNOW THIS: PLANT TRANSPIRATION

Plant transpiration is the process by which plants open their pores to take in carbon dioxide for photosynthesis and lose water to evaporation.

218 WORD UP!: RESPIRATION

Respiration is when a living organism takes in oxygen and releases carbon dioxide to make energy to run its body functions.

219 USE SCHOOL GROUNDS TO LEARN ABOUT NATURE

Many schools have wetlands on their properties, even if it is just a small wet area with cattails. There can be some interesting life cycles going on there. Ask your teacher if your class can go out to look around on school grounds for signs of animals (or plants) in the spring and see what's there. You might find some interesting things!

Go to the EPA site and learn about how your class can participate in the "Adopt-a-Wetland" program at *www.epa.gov/region4/water/ wetlands/education/adopt.html*.

220 SPREAD THE WORD ABOUT: WETLANDS

People used to think that wetlands were wasted land. Developers would drain them with ditches, fill them in with tons of soil, and build houses, schools, and parking areas on them. Then scientists began to realize the important role wetlands played in the environment.

Wetlands act like giant sponges during storms. They soak up extra storm water and afterward release it, slowly, back into the water cycle. This helps prevent flooding. Towns where people have drained wetlands have found that in a big storm, their streets and homes are often flooded because there are no wetlands to soak up the excess water.

221 CREATE A "FLOOD"

How do wetlands protect towns from flooding? To test this you will need two pie or cake pans, a ½ cup measuring cup, a damp sponge, and some water.

1. Lay the two pans next to each other. Wring out the sponge so that it has no excess water. Then place it in the center of one of the pans.

2. Pour ½ cup water into the empty pan. Notice how it covers the bottom of the pan. Now pour ½ cup water into the second pan right onto the sponge.

3. What is the difference in the water level of the two pans? Imagine that these pans are each small valleys with tiny towns. The pan without the sponge would be underwater. How would the town with the sponge fare? Towns with wetlands are the like the pan with the sponge. Wetlands take on and hold excess water in a storm and release it slowly without flooding.

222 DID YOU KNOW WETLANDS CAN ACT AS GIANT FILTERS?

Wetlands also act as giant filters, absorbing and dissolving pollutants over time. Though wetlands can become polluted from dumping, wastewater, and fertilizer runoff from farm fields, they are able to process some pollutants over time because of all the microorganisms and plants living there.

Wetlands are especially important for providing homes and breeding grounds to millions of birds, fish, and amphibians worldwide. Many wetlands have become national wildlife refuges, where you can go to take pictures and look at birds and animals.

223 SHARE THIS ECO-STORY: THE EVERGLADES

The Everglades are a huge wetland that once covered more than 4 million acres of southern Florida. Sometimes called the "river of grass," the Everglades grew from a shallow sheet of water that slowly flowed across a grassy plain. In the late 1800s, people began draining parts of the Everglades for development. Roads were built and towns sprang up. The Everglades shrank to half its original size. Cities like Miami flourished where a thriving wetland once stood. Sewage and waste from the cities was pumped into the remaining wetlands. Over time, scientists began to see the importance of the Everglades. Even with its smaller size, the Everglades filtered the pollutants coming from the cities, absorbing the worst of it like a sewage treatment plant. During storms the Everglades protected the cities from storm surge flooding. People also travel to the Everglades to experience its vast array of wildlife.

Now there is a big effort to protect what is left of the Everglades. Thousands of acres of manmade treatment marshes have been planted between the cities and the Everglades. They use native plants to naturally clean harmful nutrients from water flowing into the Everglades. Farmers have had to change the pesticides and fertilizers they use, knowing now that they will eventually flow with the water into the Everglades. Hopefully over time, the Everglades' many endangered animals will begin to thrive again and this unique and beneficial wetland can be preserved for all time.

224 SHARE THIS ECO-FACT: THE PLANT CURE

One of the sad effects of cutting down the rainforests is that scientists believe many of the plants found in them hold the key to curing human diseases. As a matter of fact, almost half of the drugs made in the United States comes from the work done on wild plants. Some plant cures are simply amazing! Aspirin, which cures headaches and lowers fevers, is made from salicylic acid, an extract from the bark of willow trees.

225 SHOW RESPECT FOR FLOWERS!

Before scientists discovered the medicine that could be made from the rosy periwinkle, 90 percent of all children who got childhood leukemia died from it. Then in the 1960s, scientists began testing the small, pink flower from Madagascar. They discovered that extracts from the plant had great healing effects. Now children have a 90 percent recovery rate from leukemia instead of 10 percent. All from a little pink flower from the rainforests of Madagascar! To the children infected with that terrible disease, the rosy periwinkle is a miracle drug.

Other examples are just as stunning. As early as the 1700s, a doctor and botanist named William Wuthering discovered that when he ground up leaves of the wildflower foxglove and gave it to a patient, it would cause his heart to beat harder. When he gave it to people in the middle of heart failure, the drug made their heart beat strongly again! This wildflower became a heart drug called digitalis that is still in use today.

226 FIND A BOOK ABOUT: JOHN MUIR

Sometimes a great environmentalist does their job just by telling stories. That was John Muir's gift. Through the stories he wrote about his life in the Sierra Nevada Mountains of California, he affected millions of people. Muir (1838-1914), one of our earliest conservationists, started the Sierra Club, an important conservation organization, and helped to save the Yosemite Valley and other wilderness areas. He believed that we needed to save wilderness not for its money value or even its biodiversity, but for its own sake and for its spiritual effect on mankind. He helped to change the way we look at the natural world.

227 LEARN ABOUT: JULIA HILL

In 1997 a young woman named Julia Butterfly Hill climbed into a giant redwood that was going to be cut down and refused to come down. She stayed in the tree (named Luna) for two years! She finally came down when an agreement could be reached with the lumber company not to cut the tree down.

228 TRANSPLANT A TREE

You can also transplant little trees that have seeded in your yard or a vacant lot nearby. These are baby trees that will not make it because they are in the shadow of bigger trees or will be cut down when the town mows. Fill a paper cup with soil and, using a little garden shovel, dig around the roots of your baby tree and plant it in your cup. Make sure the roots are pointing down and water the tree well. Then place it on your windowsill in the sun until you are ready to replant it.

Be sure to keep a journal on your tree's progress. Make note of how often you water it, how much sun it receives, and so on. If your tree doesn't grow well, you can go back to your notes and try replanting, but this time change something in your plan. You could also bring your notes to a nursery and talk to someone there about what you may have done too much or too little of, in trying to grow your tree.

Be patient, and stick with it, because even though a mighty forest begins with one little seed, it doesn't grow overnight!

229 PICK THE RIGHT SPOT FOR TREES

When you are ready to plant your trees, pick the right spots for them. Trees grow very tall and spread out. Look at the trees in your neighborhood. See how big they get? Make sure to plant your trees at least ten feet apart and in a place where they will get plenty of sun.

- Dig a hole that gives plenty of room for your tree's roots to point down and spread out.
- Loosen the soil all around the hole so the tiny roots can grow quickly.

- Pour some water in the bottom of the hole.
- Set the tree in the hole with the roots down and fill all around it with the dug-up dirt. You can add compost to the soil to help give it a healthy start.
- Water your tree generously. If it doesn't rain in the next few days, you should water the trees by hand to get them off to a good start.
- Check on your trees often. You can feel good knowing that someday you will sit in the shade of your trees. You have done the earth a kind service.

CHAPTER 6

ENERGY AND POWER

230 WOULD YOU CHANGE YOUR ENERGY USE?

If you knew how much energy it took to make things, would you try to use less stuff? You might be surprised to learn the high energy cost of the things you use every day. These estimates alone might make you go green, and that's a good thing! Here are some things you should know:

231 WHAT HAPPENS WHEN YOU FLUSH?

A regular toilet uses eight gallons of water every time you flush. It's estimated that every day Americans use 4.8 billion gallons of clean water just to flush their toilets. That's almost half the water we use indoors every day!

232 CHOOSE DIFFERENT PAPER TOWELS!

If every home in America bought just one roll of 100 percent recycled paper towels, it would save more than a half million trees.

233 THINK ABOUT THAT OLD TV!

Every year we throw away 20 million tons of electronics, such as old computers, radios, and CD and MP3 players.

234 WHAT YOUR SCHOOL SPENDS

Most schools spend more money paying for energy, like electricity and heat, than they do on school supplies.

235 SHARE THIS ECO-FACT: SOLAR ENERGY

Solar energy is a "renewable resource." This means that you can use it, and more is being made all the time. As long as the sun is shining, more energy will be there for us to use. Solar energy is collected for heating homes, businesses, and water. It's used to dry out agricultural grains like wheat and corn, herbs, and fruit. People use solar power to heat pools, greenhouses, and arboretums. Solar power charges emergency phones on American highways, keeps streetlights lit, and powers flashing road signs. Builders have even developed solar roof shingles!

236 DO RESEARCH ON: PHOTOVOLTAICS

Solar power can even be made into electricity. Solar cell technology that does this is called "photovoltaic." Photovoltaic energy is when sunlight is collected by a "solar cell" and then passed through a special "semiconductor" to create an electrical flow. This advance was actually discovered accidentally—by researchers at a telephone company in 1954 who were looking at how silicon reacted to sunlight.

237 GET TO KNOW: ULTRAVIOLET LIGHT

Ultraviolet light is a kind of electromagnetic radiation from the sun that has a wavelength shorter than visible light, so we cannot see it. Though too much ultraviolet light is bad for us, we do need some to be healthy.

238 MEMORIZE THIS: SUBLIMATION

Sublimation is when ice evaporates directly into vapor without first melting into the water phase.

239 KNOW THIS: SEMICONDUCTOR

A semiconductor is a material that can carry the electrical charge made by the sunlight, allowing us to use energy from the sun. Most solar semiconductors are a layer of silicon.

240 LEARN THIS ECO-TERM: FLUORESCENT LAMPS

Fluorescent lamps are very special lightbulbs that burn cooler and use less energy than regular bulbs. These days, you and your family can find these lamps and lightbulbs in stores everywhere. More and more people are finding that they're not only going green by using these bulbs, but they're saving money on their utility bills!

241 WORD UP!: WATT

A watt is a unit of power and how we measure electricity. A regular lightbulb usually uses between 40 and 100 watts of electricity. The 100-watt bulb is brighter and uses more units of power.

242 DO A SOLAR ENERGY EXPERIMENT

The only problem with solar power is that it's not always sunny outside! Some places have more cloud cover that blocks sunlight, and of course no solar power is collected at night. The ideal place for solar power is an area where there is little cloud cover—such as a desert or other arid region—and which has the space needed for solar collectors to lie out and take in the sunshine. In the United States, the southwestern part of the country has the sunniest climate, making it an excellent location for solar collection. But homes everywhere can benefit from some solar collection. Even something as simple as big, south-facing windows can bring solar heat into a home. This is called "passive solar" collection.

Stand in front of a window directly in the sun (this works in winter or summer). You can feel the heat from the sun on your skin, even though you are behind glass. If you keep standing there, you will feel hotter and hotter. Stay as long as you can until you start to feel sweat break out on your skin. Now step away from the window into the shade. Can you feel the temperature difference?

243 SUPPORT SOLAR SCIENCE!

The other problem with solar power is that you need a big area facing the sun to collect it. On a single home, the collection area can be on a rooftop facing the sun, but what about a tall building with many apartments? Or a whole city? It takes space to collect solar power. It is difficult for big power companies to collect and sell solar power because sunlight collection takes a lot of space. There were only fourteen known large, solar electric generating units working in the United States in 2004, all of them in the sunny states of California and Arizona.

Solar scientists have also only worked out how to convert about 25 percent of the sunlight we get into power. Plus the silicon and metals in solar cells are very stiff and hard, so they can't be used for a lot of things that aren't flat. New plastic semiconductors are much more flexible and easier to make, but they only make 10 percent of the sunlight available into power. Solar science still has a long way to go to be the endless, clean, free power we hope it will be, but it's getting there!

244 SPREAD THE WORD ABOUT: WIND ENERGY

The wind is renewable energy because it never stops blowing! It flows around the planet pushed on by the uneven heating and cooling of the earth's surface. It is an endless supply of power, if only we can harness it.

As soon as men took to the ocean in boats they began using wind power for sailing. Farmers fastened early wind turbines onto windmills. They used them to grind grain and pull up water from wells. Even early lumber mills were powered by windmills. In the early 1900s, when electricity had not made it out to rural ranches in the American west, ranchers put up small windmills to generate their own electricity. Nowadays, wind energy is mostly used for creating electricity. The turning blades power a generator that turns the mechanical power into electricity. Modern windmills are called wind machines, and they are gigantic. One wind machine can be as tall as a twenty-story building with three blades that are 200 feet long. They are placed in wide, open areas, often near the coast, where the wind blows a lot of the time, or across vast expanses of uninhabited areas in the Midwest.

More and more states are starting to make wind farms to help supply people with the electricity they need. The state of California makes more than twice as much wind power as any of the other thirty states using it. But they only work when the wind is blowing!

245 UNDERSTAND: WIND FARMS

Wind farms with dozens of wind machines can make electricity for entire communities. A wind farm in Texas has forty-six wind machines that make enough electricity for 7,300 homes. Wind farms are usually owned by people or businesses, which then sell the power to public power companies. In the United States today, wind machines are making enough electricity to supply about 1.6 million homes with energy. That may sound like a lot, but in a country as big as ours, it still accounts for less than 1 percent of the population. That number is growing over time, though. In just the last ten years, the amount of wind power being generated has grown 300 percent.

246 VISIT A WIND FARM

Because of the wind stirred up off the ocean, many wind farms are being planned for offshore sites. The first offshore wind farm in the United States is planned for off the coast of Cape Cod, Massachusetts. According to wind power experts, each windmill will be able to make up to 4 million kilowatt hours (kWh) of electricity per year. That will supply up to 400 homes with energy.

247 HAVE A WINDMILL PARTY

All you need to have a windmill party are squares of paper 8.5" x 8.5" (hint: You can use regular copy paper and cut 2.5 inches off the end to make it square. This is a great way to use up junk mail paper that hasn't been folded.) You will need enough squares of paper, thumbtacks, and pencils for each person making a windmill. You will also need some scissors and an adult helper to use them.

1. After your grownup helper has cut your squares, have everyone color their squares on both sides, with markers or crayons.
2. Ask your grownup helper to cut each square four times, one cut from each corner into about 1 inch from the center.
3. Have everyone take their thumbtack and push it into the pencil just below the metal band below the eraser. Now pull it out again. That hole is where you will attach your windmill.
4. To fold your windmill, hold your newly cut square in your left hand between your thumb and forefinger. Try to keep your thumb right in the middle of the square (you'll have to push your hand down into one of the cuts to reach the center with your thumb)
5. With your right hand take the right corner of each cut section and fold over in an arch to the center, trapping the tip under your thumb. (Don't crease the paper.)
6. Do this for all four sections. You have to keep all four tips under your thumb. This is a little tricky, especially if you all start giggling!

7. Now take your thumbtack and push it through all four tips and the center of your paper and pin it back into your pencil. You may need some help from your grownup helper.

8. You have made a windmill. Take it outside into the wind and watch it spin!

248 DO RESEARCH ON: WATER POWER

Power from water can be made in many different ways, the most common being with a hydroelectric dam. This is where a river is blocked until the water builds up into a large lake, or reservoir, behind a tall dam wall. The water is released through an opening over the dam and as it falls, it flows through a machine called a turbine and turns the propellers attached to an electric generator. This creates the electricity. The greater height from which the water falls, the more power it makes.

Natural waterfalls such as Niagara Falls work in much the same way. The power created by the falling water makes the generator work, which makes the electricity. It is gravity working on the water that gives us this power. Power lines connected to the generator carry the electricity where it needs to go.

Hyrdoelectric power is a clean and renewable power source. There is no pollution given off while using hydroelectric power. The reservoir behind the dam can be a place for people to swim, boat, and fish. Farmers can use some of the water for irrigation of their fields. A dam, once built, can last for 100 years.

There are a few bad things about dams that are important to know. To build a hydroelectric dam, a large area must be flooded behind the dam to make the reservoir. Whole communities sometimes have to be moved to another place. Entire forests can be drowned. Rotting vegetation under the water can give off methane. The water released from the dam can be colder than usual and this can affect the ecosystems in the rivers downstream. It can also cause erosion downstream, washing away riverbanks and scraping away life on the river bottoms. The worst effect of dams has been observed on salmon that have to travel upstream to spawn, or lay their eggs. If blocked by a dam, the salmon life cycle (and that of many other fish) cannot be completed. To try to solve this, fish experts have designed fish ladders to get fish over the dam. A fish ladder (also called a fish way or fish pass) is a manmade structure built around a dam to allow fish to still make their way upstream to spawn. They are often a chain of low steps up, which the fish can leap. The flow of water has to be just right to attract fish to the ladder but not tire them out.

249 KNOW THE INS AND OUTS OF TIDE POWER

Other forms of water power include capturing the energy of the rising and falling tides. In some ways, tide power is more dependable than wind and solar power because the tides go in and out all day and night at a rate we can anticipate. Though tides never change, the amount of water moving back and forth does increase during storms and, because they are controlled by the moon's gravity, the tides do differ according to the phase of the moon. People have been using the tides to power little coastal mills to grind grain for generations.

250 TEACH YOURSELF ABOUT: WATER WHEELS

Another form of water power is a simple water wheel placed in a river. The water flowing down stream turns the wheel and generates power. The water wheel has been used to mill grains, mine ore, pump water, and power iron forges for more than 1,000 years.

251 TURN THE LIGHTS OFF!

There are many ways you can save energy at home. Some are really simple—you can do them yourself with very little effort. Others will need help from your parents. Try a few and see how easy it is to act green! First, this one is really simple—turn out lights when you are not using them.

252 GET NEW BULBS

Ask your parents to get "compact fluorescent lamps" for your lights. They use one-fourth of the electricity of a regular lightbulb, burn cooler, and last a lot longer.

253 TURN THE OTHER STUFF OFF, TOO!

Don't leave the TV on when no one is watching it. Also turn off computers, radios, stereos, electric blankets, and heating pads when not in use.

254 FIREPLACES CAN BE GREAT—IF YOU'RE SMART!

In the winter, ask your parents to close the damper in your fireplace when you are not using it. Heat rises and can escape right out of your chimney! Fireplaces can be a great way to naturally heat the house, just make sure one of your parents is tending to it and making sure to minimize heat loss through the flue!

255 PUT ON A SWEATER!

Ask your parents to turn the heat down just a couple of degrees in the winter and wear a sweater while you're inside. Or you can ask them to use a ceiling fan on less hot days in the summer instead of air conditioning.

256 STOP PERUSING AND CLOSE THAT DOOR!

It's tempting to stand at the refrigerator and scan the shelves and door for what looks just right, but think about all that cold air coming out! Next time, take a quick look—or even better, know what you want before you get in there. Get it and close the door quickly. It's these little things that all add up and help save energy in the long run.

257 SOLAR LIGHTS ARE JUST RIGHT

Why keep those walkways lit the whole day and night? Ask your mom or dad to get solar lights for your outdoor walkways. They are charged by the sun during the day and light your yard electricity-free at night.

258 THROW BAD AND OLD STUFF AWAY

"Detox" your house. If you can see old paint cans in the basement, old pesticide boxes in the garden shed, or old toxic household cleaners under the sink, you can call the landfill and ask when they have toxic waste pickup days. It's better to have them out of the house!

259 WIPE YOUR FACE THE EARTH-FRIENDLY WAY

Ask your parents if you can get cloth napkins to replace the paper napkins you use every day. Or get some for your mom or dad as a gift. It doesn't add much to laundry but it saves a lot of trees! By that same token, handkerchiefs save a lot of tissues and make good gifts, too.

260 CHECK THIS OUT: BULBS

If your parents replaced just one regular lightbulb in your house with a compact fluorescent lamp, they would save $30 in electricity costs over the life of that bulb. You would also stay cooler in the summer, because these bulbs give off 70 percent less heat.

261 STOP HEATING THE OUTDOORS

Has your mom or dad ever told you to close the door in the winter because you were letting all the heat out? It's true that the heat will escape out your open door, but a lot of heat sneaks out of your house through cracks you may not even realize are there. Researchers have found that people lose one-tenth of their homes' heat through little spaces they can fix. You can test for heat leaks with your fingertips. Run your fingers around the edges of your windows. Do you feel a cold spot? That window may need a little sealing to block the cold from getting in. Now run your fingers along the bottom of your doors to the outside. Do you feel cold air? That's a common place for cold leaks.

262 MAKE A DRAFT STOPPER

You can stop heat from getting out under your doors and cold from sneaking in. Get an old pillowcase from your parent and cut it into 6" wide, two-layer thick strips. Sew up both the long sides using small stitches. Then turn it inside out, so your stitches are on the inside. Now fill it with sand (your parents can buy sand from a hobby shop, nursery, or garden store). Sew up the little end. Now you can decorate your draft stopper with fabric paint. Make flowers or rainbows to remind you that summer will be back soon!

263 SHARE THIS ECO-FACT: METHANE ENERGY

Methane gas adds to the greenhouse effect in the atmosphere, but it also can be collected and burned for energy. It is now fueling some passenger trains and buses in Sweden. Called "biogas," this new form of energy is created by processing waste, like animal parts left over at the butcher, to produce methane. It is considered a green energy source. Methane is made by mixing a big organic soup with all the leftover cow parts and manure, and then adding bacteria that will digest the mixture. The bacteria, as it digests, gives off the gas. The energy company then collects the methane and sells it as fuel. Each cow can provide 2.5 miles of train travel. That's no bull!

CHAPTER 7

RECYCLE!

264 RECYCLING PLASTIC IS FANTASTIC!

Recycle plastic bottles and jugs so they don't find their way into rivers, streams, and the ocean. It's not difficult to recycle—everyone can do it, anywhere. Even if you see a bottle on the sidewalk or in the park, why not pick it up, bring it home, and recycle it? Recycling is such an easy way to do your part. If only everyone would recycle!

265 RECYCLE REFRIGERANTS

Ask your parents to make sure that before they throw away old refrigerators, air conditioners, and dehumidifiers, they have the refrigerants recovered and recycled and not released into the air. (They can do this by asking the local trash collector if the refrigerant will be recovered and recycled before the appliance is thrown away.)

266 SHARE THIS ECO-FACT: TISSUES

If every home in the United States bought one box of 100 percent recycled tissues, we could save more than 87,000 trees! We could also stop more than 300 garbage trucks full of trash (in tissues) from going to the landfills.

267 RECYCLE AND REUSE

Make recycling boxes for paper, magazines, newspaper, cardboard, cans, and bottles. Then be sure to use them! This is another really easy way to recycle that we should all be doing! If you see your family members, peers, or friends *not* using recycling methods like these, why not ask nicely that they do so?

268 BE NUMBER ONE (OR TWO)

Ask your parents to try to buy products that come in plastics with the #1 or #2 marked on the bottom. These are recyclables. Try not to buy products sold in plastic bottles marked with a #3, #4, #5, #6, and especially #7. You can help by going along on the next shopping trip and helping your parents look at the recycling numbers.

269 YES, YOU CAN!

Recycle bottles and cans. Help out your parents by returning bottles and cans that have deposits. If you don't have time, bag them all up and bring them to the local Boy/Girl Scout or school bottle drive bins.

270 BAG IT

Help your parents recycle shopping bags at your local grocery store. Do you and your family have a cabinet full of old bags? Why not bring those same ones back to the store and use them again? What else are you going to do with them?

271 MOO FOR #2

Buy milk and juice in #2 plastic jugs and recycle them. Waxed cartons often cannot be recycled.

If your city or town recycles, they should have information to send you about what can and cannot be recycled in your area. Sometimes, this information comes in the form of a handy sheet that you could stick to your refrigerator. Be sure to have this information close by and check it if you are unsure about whether or not something can be recycled in your town. There should also be a phone number your parents can call, in case you have any more questions.

272 BOX LUNCH IS BEST!

Buy a lunch box and use it all year, instead of bringing lunches every day in paper or plastic bags. And lunch boxes can be cool! Personalize yours with stickers or drawings. Not only is it green but it's yours, and yours only! Here's an idea, why not design it with green logos and emblems? Spread your message in the lunchroom!

273 GRAB THAT BAG

Bring your own canvas bags to the grocery store to pack your food in. These days, many grocery stores and supermarkets offer such bags for sale. You can keep one in your car, next to your door (if you walk to the store), or roll one up and ask your mom to keep it in her purse. These bags don't take much space and can unroll to a large, sturdy bag. Some grocery stores even give you and your family incentives to bring your own bag. Some stores offer money if you use canvas bags, while others sponsor contests for savvy shoppers who avoid plastic and paper bags.

274 THINK INK

People use a lot of ink cartridges in their computer printers. You can now recycle them through your local post office. Clear, plastic, stamped envelopes are available for you to send each cartridge in after it is empty. It won't cost you a penny!

Talk to your parents about any office supply stores in your area that may accept old computer ink cartridges or even give you a coupon to buy something in the store!

275 DONATE A PHONE

You can donate old cell phones to people who need them. For information on how to do it, look at *www.wirelessrecycling.com*.

Another good place to look for this information is your town or city hall, or your local post office. Sometimes there is information there about donating phones to people serving in the military.

276 COMPUTE THIS!

Even your old computers can be recycled. Donate your old computers that still work to your local school or daycare center. If they don't work, you can recycle them through electronics recycling companies that will even pick them up at your home. Look online for "computer recycling."

277 THINK GLOBAL, ACT LOCAL

Call your local recycling, solid waste, or public works departments to find out what recycling programs are offered in your town.

278 TALK UP YOUR TRASH COLLECTOR!

Ask your trash collector or at the local landfill about recycling in your area. Your state's environmental agency can help you find more information about local and regional recycling programs. To find out who and where they are, check this website: *www.epa.gov/msw/states.htm*.

279 WASH CYCLE RECYCLE

If you are trying to recycle a big item, like a washing machine, call the store where it came from for information about how to recycle it. You local town's garbage department might also be able to help you figure out how to dispose of large items.

280 SURF THIS!

If you want to recycle electronic equipment, like computers, you can go to this website: *www.nrc-recycle.org/resources/electronics/index.htm*.

281 MAKE COOL ART PAPER

Making your own paper can be fun and the results are really cool. To start you'll need a large square pan, about three inches deep (like a lasagna pan), a used paper grocery bag (reused until it starts to tear), a square of fine mesh window screen that will fit into the pan, a rolling pin, newspaper to work on, a blender, and an adult to run the blender.

1. Tear the bag into tiny pieces.
2. Put the pieces and three cups of warm water into the blender, cover it, and turn it on medium speed for about five seconds until the paper is pulp.
3. Put the screen in the bottom of the pan and cover it with 1 inch of water.
4. Pour about a cup of the pulp over the screen and spread it around with your fingers.

5. Lift the screen carefully out of the pan and let the water drain away.

6. Then set it on an open section of newspaper. Close the newspaper over the top of the pulp. Flip it over so that the pulp is now face down.

7. Use the rolling pin to roll out the extra water. Open the newspaper and carefully peel off the screen.

8. Let the pulp dry overnight. In the morning, peel your new sheet of paper off the newspaper. You have just recycled paper. Now paint something cool on it.

282 START PAPER RECYCLING AT SCHOOL

Schools use tons of paper. They are good places to save a lot of paper . . . and trees! Talk to your teacher about your recycling idea. If your teacher likes the idea, have everyone in your class bring in a cardboard box with the top flaps cut off. Decorate the boxes drawing colorful trees, flowers, mountains, and lakes. Then write in big letters, "Save Trees—Recycle!" Deliver them around the school to the classes that want them. Collect ten cool facts about trees to give out with your recycling boxes to get people motivated. You can start with the ones found in this book! Start a contest to see which class can recycle the most paper. This might motivate kids to help out. Give out baby trees as prizes!

283 GET LESS MAIL

Though recycling is good, not all states have great recycling programs, so it's good to reduce how much junk mail you get in the first place. Here are a few things you and your parents can do to help. To stop getting junk catalogs, make a pile of all your unwanted catalogs and ask your parents to take a few minutes every week and call the toll free numbers on each one and ask that their names (on the mailing label) be removed from the company's mailing list. You can also send a note to the Direct Marketing Association. For $1, they will remove your names from their national database for five years. Make sure you give them everyone's name in your family who gets junk mail, spelled in every way you get them on labels (they are often misspelled). Send your letter to: DMA Mail Preference Service, P.O. Box 643, Carmel, NY 10512. You can read more about this at: *www.DMAConsumers.org*.

284 GET IN THE LOOP!

Americans use a lot of stuff in our everyday lives. If everyone recycled, we would produce a lot less garbage and use a lot fewer resources. Recycling works in a loop, but it only works if all parts of the loop function. The first part of the loop is when people, like you, recycle paper, bottles, cans, and plastics. The next part is when the recycled things get collected, cleaned, and sold to factories that can use them. Then the recyclables are made into new products like newspapers, carpets, and plastic tubs. Then people, like you and your family, buy them again! That is the recycling loop. Whenever you buy a recycled product you are helping close the recycling loop. By recycling just 4 feet of paper, you could save one tree. If everyone in the United States recycled their newspaper just one day a week, we would save about 36 million trees a year. That's a whole forest! According to the Environmental Protection Agency (EPA), in 2005, Americans who recycled and composted stopped 64 million tons of stuff from going to landfills or being burned. That's 174 billion pounds of trash in one year alone! Recycling has an effect, and every little bit helps.

285 SHARE THIS ECO-STORY: RECYCLING

Americans recycled and conserved when we entered World War II in Europe, which lasted from 1939–1945. During that period, some products, such as meat, coffee, sugar, and tires, became in short supply. But after the war, people became richer and they stopped worrying about resources as much. It was more than twenty years before people began to think "green" again. In the 1960s, the environmental movement started making people aware of how we were altering the environment by throwing away too much stuff. People became more aware about littering, saving energy, growing organic foods, and recycling. But it would be another twenty years before it got expensive to take garbage to the landfills. That was what really got many people recycling. Today, a lot of Americans do recycle. The EPA calculates that Americans recycle about one-third of their waste. Though recycling has increased, it is not something people are required to do. There is a lot more that people can do to conserve and reuse the Earth's valuable resources.

286 CHOOSE WISELY: PAPER OR PLASTIC?

If you have gone food shopping then you have probably heard the check-out person ask, "Paper or Plastic?" The best answer, of course, is neither. If you can, you should bring your own tote bags to the grocery store instead of using so many shopping bags every week. If you have to choose, though, which shopping bag is worse for the environment? Paper bags are made from natural fibers that come from lumber waste. Plastic bags are made from the waste that is left over when oil is cleaned. Paper bags, if left out in the sun and rain, will break down or "biodegrade." Plastic bags will last for a very long time even if left out in sun and rain.

Even knowing all of this, plastic shopping bags are still thought to be better for the environment than paper shopping bags. How can this be? Well, let's compare them. Research has shown that making paper bags from trees grown on plantations takes more energy than making plastic bags from oil refinery waste. Paper bags take up about seven times the space of plastic bags and require more energy and cost to ship to stores. Paper bags take up much more room in the landfills than plastic. Paper may break down faster than plastic, but only if it is exposed to the elements. In a packed and covered landfill, paper bags will last a long time, too. Overall, it is best to bring your own shopping bags to the grocery store if you can. Store them under the seat in your car for easy access the next time you shop. If you do take paper or plastic shopping bags from the store, save them and use them until they fall apart. Or find creative ways to reuse them—paper grocery bags are great for covering schoolbooks. Ask your grocery store to make available a collection bin for used plastic bags.

287 PUT PRESSURE ON COMPANIES

Write to the companies that make your favorite foods and ask them to switch to recyclable containers. Consumers do have power!

288 CHECK THIS OUT: CATALOGS

More than 17 billion catalogs are sent out in the United States every year. That is more than sixty-four catalogs for every person in the country, including kids!

Sometimes a catalog company will even send you two copies of the same catalog, which is especially wasteful!

If a catalog comes to your house and your family never buys anything from it, suggest to your Mom and Dad that you contact the company and discontinue the catalog. Sometimes companies send catalogs without even being requested to. It makes sense to conserve and stop receiving the catalogs you do not want.

289 RECYCLE CATALOGS

Before you recycle your junk catalogs, make sure your recycling center takes them. If they do, recycle them with your glossy magazines. If they don't, find a second home for them. Keep them out of the landfill by asking at school if you can put them in the teacher's lounge, or maybe the art teacher can use them for art projects. Ask your recycling center to start taking them, too. It can't hurt to ask!

290 GIVE SPRAY PAINT THE BRUSH-OFF

Instead of buying paint in a spray can, which can't be recycled, buy a can of paint and a paintbrush. Make sure, when you are done with it that you throw away the can in a safe place. If you aren't sure where to dispose of aerosol cans, ask the people at your town landfill.

291 WASTE NOT, WANT NOT

Try not to buy products with a lot of extra packaging, like plastic trays inside boxes with extra plastic wrapping. All that packaging uses resources and just has to be thrown away or recycled in the end anyway!

292 SHOP CO-OP

Join and shop at your local food co-op. You can buy food in bulk with little or no packaging at all.

293 SPREAD RECYCLING KNOW-HOW

You might be confused about how to recycle certain things. Learn what items are the most difficult to recycle and how to do it. Make a list and post it at your school—this will help others know that there are places for recycling a lot of things that might have ended up at the landfill. Write a letter to the editor of your local paper telling everyone what they can recycle and how.

CHAPTER 8

AT HOME, AT SCHOOL, AND BEYOND

294 GET TO KNOW: GREEN HOMES

When people build "green homes" they take extra effort to build in ways their home will help them save resources over time. They often use materials that are recycled and safer to live with.

295 CHECK THIS OUT: EURO-GREEN

The European government lets people pay lower taxes if they make their homes more energy efficient.

Do you think your government should do this? Talk to your parents about writing a letter to an elected representative expressing your opinion and support for more environmentally friendly policies. Maybe you could start a petition in your neighborhood: a petition is a piece of paper that people sign to express support for an idea or a program. You have to go door to door to ask people for their signature, but if you collect lots of signatures and send it to an elected representative in the government, they really do take notice!

296 GO LOW-FLOW!

Here are some of the things people put in a green home. Share these ideas with your parents. You should look into low-flow showers, toilets, and washers that use less water.

297 THINK WINDOWS AND WIN

Ever thought that adding big south-facing windows with insulated shades might save on heat and light? It sure will!

298 INSULATE AND BE GREAT

Good insulation made from recycled paper cellulose will trap heat inside in the winter and keep it outside in the summer—what a great concept!

299 SOLAR PANEL PATROL

Solar panels for heating water and radiant heat floors will offer your family all the heat they need directly from the sun! While solar panels might be a bit expensive to buy and install, they will more than pay for

all that hard effort in the long run in the money and energy you save!
Try to convince your parents to make this worthwhile buy.

300 RECYCLED ROOFING—WHY NOT?

If your family is building or renovating, you all should think about recycled
plastic carpets, decks, and even roof tiles. Bet you didn't even know
you could use recycled materials for roofs, carpet, and, decks!

301 GARDEN GREEN, TOO

Certain plants are better than others for your garden and the earth.
In fact, landscaping with native plants that don't need extra water or
any fertilizer is the best way to go! So if someone else in your family is
the gardener or if it's you, why not consider growing local favorites?

302 DESIGN YOUR IDEAL GREEN HOUSE

Just for fun, design the perfect green house. Take a big sheet of paper
and draw your ideal house. Add a windmill in the yard and solar panels
on the roof. Make a garden with vegetables and plants that would live
in your climate. You can make it really fun and have it be in a tree or built
into the side of a hill. Show the inside rooms with big solar windows,
plants, and a recycling pantry. Make your room really cool, too!

Be sure to show your drawing to your parents. Some of your ideas may be too fantastic or too expensive to do, but you never know until you ask! And maybe the fun of looking at your drawing will get your parents thinking about what they can do to make your home more energy-efficient. You might remind your parents that increasing the energy efficiency of your home may increase its value.

The projects you can undertake to make your house—or even just one room—more eco-friendly and energy-efficient may be small, but they will have very large effects. Or the project could be a big one that you and your whole family do together.

303 MAKE YOUR YARD GREEN

If you want to live green and save energy, there are many things you can do around the house and yard. Offer to rake the yard, walks, and driveway for your parents and neighbors so no one needs to use electrical equipment like leaf-blowers. Machines use a lot of energy and the wind will bring those leaves back anyway! If your yard is small, you can use a push mower instead of a gas mower. Raking and hand mowing is actually kind of fun and it is really good exercise, too.

304 COOL IT ON COOLANT

Coolant is a fluid agent (gas or liquid) that produces cooling, especially one used to cool a system by transferring heat away from one part to another.

Ask your parents to make sure your air conditioners are in good condition and aren't leaking coolant, because coolant isn't good for the soil or the water.

305 GET YOUR AIR IN GOOD CONDITION

When your parents buy a new air conditioner, ask them to buy one that uses non–ozone-depleting refrigerant (the coolant used in refrigerators). Tell Mom and Dad: please no R-22 refrigerant! And ask your parents to make sure that when their car air conditioner gets serviced, the refrigerants are recovered and recycled, not released into the air.

306 JOIN A GREEN GROUP

There are many great environmental groups that you and your family can join. Ask for a membership for your birthday and give them to others as gifts. You can start by looking at the websites of these organizations to see if what they do is the kind of work you'd like to support. Some groups work to save all wildlife, while others focus on birds or a specific kind of animal. Some groups save all habitats, while others pay attention to just rainforests or deserts or grasslands or the ocean. Some groups work on behalf of the environment in Washington, D.C. to change and enforce environmental laws.

307 CLEAN GREEN

Ask your parents to buy biodegradable cleaning products so that cleaning your house doesn't hurt the soil and water system.

You can also talk to your parents about finding out if there are cleaners you can make at home, without any chemicals or toxins. For example, did you know that if you have silver jewelry, you can clean it just as easily with a toothbrush and toothpaste, as with silver polish? There are many handy household tips like this to help you clean things without having to buy fancy products from a store. Have fun with your Mom or Dad investigating these tips and trying them out.

308 CLUBS YOU AND YOUR FAMILY CAN JOIN

Here are a few of the most common environmental groups and their websites.

- The Sierra Club works to save our national parks and wilderness areas: *www.sierraclub.org*
- The World Wildlife Fund works to protect the world's wildlife and wildlands: *www.worldwildlife.org*
- The Rainforest Alliance works to save tropical rainforests all over the world: *www.rainforest-alliance.org*
- The Nature Conservancy works to save plants and animals by protecting their habitats: *www.nature.org*
- The National Wildlife Federation works to protect nature and wildlife: *www.nwf.org*
- Greenpeace, USA works to preserve the earth and the life it supports: *www.greenpeaceusa.org*

309 START YOUR OWN GREEN GROUP!

What kinds of things do you want to do? Do you want to help save the environment or just teach other people how to think green? Do you want to focus on saving all wildlife or one kind of animal, like tigers, that you love? Once you decide on your mission you can come up with a group name and a mission statement. Your mission statement tells what you hope to do in your green group.

310 DECIDE WHAT TIME YOU CAN COMMIT

You also have to decide how much time you and your group can commit to your goals. One hour a week? Two? Make it a reasonable amount of time so everyone can make it.

Everyone in the group should have something to do to help out. Think about what skills each of the members of your group have. Is there an artist who can make posters? Is there a computer expert who can make you a website? Who wants to take notes, make phone calls, and do research online? At whose house will you meet, or will you ask to use a room in school after hours? Maybe a meeting during lunch would be fun, too. You should consider having a grownup advisor to help out.

311 KEEP MAKING PLANS!

At the end of each meeting, plan what you will do at your next meeting so everyone has something to look forward to. Make sure everyone gets a chance to speak and be heard. That is one thing that makes a group work well. Don't worry if someone misses a meeting, but maybe call her up later and tell her what she missed.

312 EXPANDING YOUR CAUSE

Decide over time if you want to invite anyone else to join the group or keep it just a friends group. If you decide that you want more members, you will have to advertise with posters or announcements at school. Creating a group and opening it to people you don't know very well is a great way to make new friends.

Do you need to raise money to do things like make fliers or give money to a cause that your group wants to help?

313 RAISE SOME "GREEN"!

Every activist group needs a bit of money. Whether it's for fliers, cookies, or something else—there are tons of ways you and your group can come up with funds. Here are some ideas about how to raise money for your group.

314 USE HOUSEHOLD "TRASH"

If there are a bunch of bottles and cans in your garage that no one plans on using, why not bring them to your local bottle exchange and get some money for them? Also, you could see if there are any old furniture, toys, or games that you could sell at a garage sale. What an easy way to save space, recycle goods, and make money!

315 WASH THOSE CARS AND BAKE THOSE COOKIES!

Another way to make money is to organize a car wash in front of your school. Charge $5 per car and put all the money in your collection. Be sure to get permission from your principal first. Or you could have a bake sale. Make it fun and stay focused on your goal by making cookies shaped like animals, mountains, and trees! Again, make sure that you have permission to use the space for wherever you want to host this bake sale. Before you know it, you will have lots of money to donate to a good cause!

316 GETTING GRANTS WITH YOUR FOLKS

Now this one might take a bit more time, effort, and teamwork—but it could really pay off! Ask your parents to help you apply for grants from local organizations. There are a lot of grants available, and if you and your group can make a good pitch to get the funds, chances are good that you can attract outside support for your very important work.

317 COUNT YOUR MILES

Scientists have worked out that it takes an acre of trees a year to absorb the carbon dioxide of a car driven 8,700 miles. How many trees does your family need to take up the carbon dioxide made from your driving? Ask your parents how many miles they each drive per year. If they don't know you can write down their mileage and check again a week later. Then multiply that by the 52 weeks in a year. The national average is about 12,000 miles per year. That's over an acre of trees per year needed to absorb the carbon dioxide, per car, on the road. That's a lot of trees!

318 WALK THE WALK

If the place you need to go is not too far from home, try walking. Walking is also good for you.

Remember that you need to be safe, too. Your environment—the area in which you live—also includes cars and other vehicles. Drivers absolutely need to be able to see you clearly when you are walking. Be sure to wear reflective clothing if you are walking after sunset, and be sure you know and understand the rules that involve pedestrians.

319 RIDE THE RIDE

Riding a bike is good, too, since it saves gas and is great exercise. It's also faster than walking. Always follow safety regulations and wear a bicycle helmet when riding. Ride bikes with friends to get to places, but also because it's just fun to ride!

320 GET TOGETHER ON RIDES

If the place you need to go is too far to walk or bike, look into public transportation. If your town has buses or trains, get to know the schedules and see how they might work for you. Ask one of your parents to ride the bus with you to a place you plan to go. See if you are comfortable riding a bus. Try it with a group of friends. Most of the time, using public transportation is a lot easier than having your parents find a parking spot.

321 MAKE ONE TRIP

Another way to save on driving is to collect the errands you have to do and make one trip for all of them. Keep a list of the things that need to be done in town, at the grocery store, or at the mall. Save them up and try to drive only once for a whole bunch of errands. Or try using stores closer to home.

322 SHARE THE RIDE

Carpooling with friends is another good way to save on driving. But don't keep your driver waiting. Idling engines use a lot of gas!

If your parents drive to work, ask them if they have looked into carpooling with other people they work with. Remind them that carpooling saves everyone money, and people who carpool can have a lot of fun by enjoying each other's company on the ride to work.

323 THINK ABOUT HOW WE USE WATER

Water may be the easiest thing in your house to use less of, because we use so much of it every day, in so many different ways. We use water to wash our cars and ourselves; we use water when our plants are thirsty, and when we are thirsty; we use water to cook, and we use it to brush our teeth after we eat. When we use so much water all of the time, we tend to take it for granted and not think that water is a resource that we should conserve whenever we can.

324 TAKE A LOOK AT THE WATER BILL

Try this: Ask one of your parents to show you the water bill. What's that—you didn't know they had to *pay* for the water that comes out of the faucet? Oh, you most certainly do, and if the water is hot, how do you think it got that way? Energy was required to make it hot, and energy costs money.

325 WHY MIGHT YOU WANT TO SAVE ON WATER?

Money your family spends on heating and water and electricity and other resources is money that doesn't get spent on vacations, clothes, toys, games, and other things you might want to buy. Now, if you end up taking some very simple steps to help conserve, your family's bills for water and heat and electricity won't be as large, and your parents will be very happy that you helped save them money!

326 FOUR WAYS TO SAVE WATER IN THE BATHROOM

1. Install low flow showerheads, toilets, and washing machines in your home.
2. Fix leaks in faucets and pipes.
3. Turn off your tap while you are brushing your teeth.
4. Take a shower instead of a bath; it uses less water.

327 TWO WAYS TO SAVE WATER WHILE DOING CHORES

1. Only wash full loads of laundry and dishes. In some machines, a half-empty load uses the same amount of water as a full load.
2. Keep cold water in a pitcher in the fridge, rather than running the tap until it gets cold.

328 TWO WAYS TO GREEN THE AREA AROUND YOU

1. Plant trees in your yard and parks that don't need watering.
2. Landscape your home, town, and parks with local species of plants that can survive without watering.

329 THINK "ALTERNATE" GARDENS

Ever thought of making a rock garden? Or perhaps a collection of driftwood or a design made by branches? You can make your garden artistic in many ways—think outside the box, or the pot, in this case!

330 TWO SMART GARDEN DECISIONS!

1. Choose drought-resistant species in case of hotter, drier times.

2. Always collect rainwater to water your gardens.

331 DID YOU KNOW? HOW DOES YOUR LAWN POLLUTE THE AIR?

Even small lawns use a lot of energy. Mowing a lawn that is only one-quarter acre makes more air pollution than driving a car from New York to Washington, D.C. and back.

332 POLLUTION AND HOW IT AFFECTS YOUR BREATHING

People in areas of high air pollution can develop breathing problems, especially kids! The World Health Organization has estimated that more than 4 million people die each year from air pollution.

333 DO RESEARCH ON: EARTH DAY

On April 22, 1970, the United States celebrated the first "Earth Day." More than 20 million people took part in all the events, which included parades, and environmental awareness talks and songs. This marked the beginning of the "environmental movement" where people began to become more aware of how we were affecting the earth. The second Earth Day was not celebrated until twenty years later, but this time more than 100 million people worldwide took part. Now people around the world celebrate Earth Day every year on April 22.

334 THROW A GREEN PARTY

This year for Earth Day have a party! Use some of the fun activities from this book as party games. Make recycled paper pinwheels. Eat earthworm dirt cups! Ask everyone to bring a can of food to donate to the local food pantry. For party favors, send everyone home with a tree seedling in a cup to plant in their yard. Saving the earth can be fun too!

One really great way to spread the word about being environmentally friendly is to have a green "block party": this is a party that everyone on your street is invited to, and everyone comes out and has a party in the street or on their lawns. By organizing a block party with a green theme, you and your family educate and inform everyone on your block at the same time!

335 MAKE EVERY DAY EARTH DAY

Earth Day is one day each year that everyone cherishes the earth. But what if we made every day Earth Day? Start an "Earth Day Every Day" club at school. Make it a lifelong habit—like brushing your teeth!

Your club could meet once a week at a different person's house and everyone could say what one thing he or she did that week to help protect the environment or conserve energy and resources. Take turns bringing in news from the newspaper or the Internet related to the environment and discuss the news with your friends. When you get together, you could do eco-friendly arts and crafts projects, like making things out of old cardboard tubes and newspaper. It could be someone's job to keep track of any Earth-friendly fairs, festivals, or activities in the community that you could all go to.

Getting together with a group of people who are all interested in the same thing makes saving the planet fun. And best of all, you learn a lot more and you come away feeling that you are helping the earth with a group of people, not just doing it all on your own!

336 MAKE SURE TO SURF GREEN

There are many cool sites online that you can check regularly for green tips. This can help you and your family to stay informed about the good things going on out there! Many times in this book you are told to find out more online. Use the computer as your resource—just don't forget to shut it off when you're done!

337 CHECK IT OUT WITH YOUR FOLKS FIRST

Always check with your parents to make sure sites are trustworthy. If you come across something that seems strange or something that surprises you, either ask your parents, turn the site off, or check that the source (who is the writer/group on the site) to make sure it's a good one!

338 WEBSITES TO SPEND SOME TIME WITH

Here are a few cool websites to check out:

- "The Green Guide," put out by the National Geographic Society, gives weekly tips about staying green. Their mission is to "inspire people to care about the planet." You can find them at *www .thegreenguide.com*.

- The Environmental Protection Agency (EPA) website tells you about ways you can be safe while protecting the environment: *www.epa.gov*.
- Campaign Earth gives tips on how you can live a greener lifestyle: *www.campaignearth.org*.

339 ENLIST THE HELP OF YOUR TEACHER

School is a great place to get other kids involved in green living. Ask your teacher if your class will study the environment in science this year and offer to help with some green projects if they relate to what you are learning.

340 BRING GREEN UP, AGAIN AND AGAIN

Even when your class is studying habitats, like rainforests, you can start talking about green topics. Share some of the activities and fun facts you learned in this book with your class.

341 BE THE ADVOCATE ON EARTH DAY!

Plan some green projects that your school can do on Earth Day.

342 BE PROUD TO BE A GREEN SCHOOL

Talk to your principal about your school becoming a "Green School." There are many advantages to becoming a Green School, like improving learning about the environment through hands-on activities to make the school more energy efficient. It can also save the school money by reducing energy costs. You can get information about becoming a Green School from the Alliance to Save Energy at *www.aoo.org*.

343 ADOPT A ROAD WITH YOUR SCHOOL

Talk to your teacher about having your class "adopt" a roadway or park to keep clean. It is a great way to take part in community service while picking up litter! Once your class does it, maybe other classes will want to adopt a road to keep clean too. Contact your county Department of Transportation for guidelines about adopting a roadway to keep clean.

344 HOLD A POSTER CONTEST

Organize and hold a "Protect the Environment" poster contest at school to raise awareness about pollution issues. Give organic chocolate as the prize.

345 GET THE WHOLE FAMILY INVOLVED!

Parents are busy. If you can help make green issues easier for them to understand, they might be happier and more willing to go green! Get your sisters and brothers involved too. Here are some things you can do to get your parents, friends, and siblings to help the environment.

346 TALK TO YOUR PARENTS ABOUT CAR USE

Ask your parents to shop online. It saves gas and time from driving to the store. Remind them that when they order they have to ask NOT to receive a printed catalog with their purchase.

Talk to your parents about making their next car an energy-efficient or hybrid car. Hybrid cars get two to three times the mileage of most cars and they are quiet, so they don't add to noise pollution. They will also save your parents money on gas.

347 BE GREEN AT THE POST OFFICE

The next time they need stamps, ask your parents to buy federal duck stamps from your local post office. These stamps support wetlands and help protect our country's bird populations.

348 COOKING SMARTS

Get your parents to thaw the meat for dinner by taking it out the night before and setting it in the fridge. This saves water by not thawing in the sink and energy by not thawing in the microwave.

349 A NEW KIND OF ORNAMENT FOR YOUR LAWN?

Talk to your parents about renewable energy. Maybe they would be interested in getting a windmill or solar panel. You never know unless you ask!

350 GREEN PETS?

You've always wanted a pet, haven't you? Or do you already have one and you're looking to get him or her a friend? Why not adopt your next pet from an animal shelter?

351 SUGGEST AND GO ON AN ECO-VACA

Take an ecological vacation. Instead of flying somewhere and staying in a hotel, go camping or hiking to a local wilderness area. It's fun and healthy and will cost a lot less than a cruise!

352 WRITE A LETTER

Write to the companies that make your favorite foods and ask them to switch to recyclable containers. Consumers do have power!

353 SPREAD THE WORD

Sometimes people don't conserve energy because they don't know how. They also may not know that they can save money by conserving. A cool poster that tells ways to conserve water, energy, gas, and resources might be a fun way to spread green thinking. Make a list of twenty easy ways to save. Ask your mom, dad, or teacher for some bigger (legal-sized) recycled paper. In big, bold letters write your title, "20 Ways to Help Save the Planet and Save Some Money Too!" Then decorate the rest of the poster with cool colors, drawings, or clipped pictures from magazines of animals or mountain scenes. Always ask permission to hang the poster at school, in the local food co-op, and other local stores.

Use your imagination to think of other ways that you could spread the word.

- If you use a device that sends text messages, try texting a friend an "Eco-Fact" from this book instead of yet another "how r u?"
- Turn things around by slipping a note into your parent's lunch and telling them what you're learning about the environment.
- Make a quiz about environmental information and turn it into a game show. Play with your friends and family. You could even have a green prize for the winner.
- Ask your parents if they would consider helping spread the green message by putting an eco-friendly bumper sticker on the family car.
- If you send e-mail, put a message at the end of every e-mail you send that says, "Before you print this e-mail, remember the environment and save paper!"
- Make a present for someone's birthday using recycled products. When the person asks you if you made it yourself, say "Yes," and tell them that the present is special because it is eco-friendly. You never know: You may encourage the person who got the gift to think about the environment and what he or she can do to go green!

- If you and your family say a prayer before a meal, be sure to remember all the things in the environment that you are grateful for. This gesture would be especially effective at Thanksgiving, when people are giving a lot of thought to what they are thankful for. When your family hears how much the environment means to you, maybe they will think harder about how they can work to be more environmentally friendly!

- Purchase thank-you cards and note cards that have been made from recycled products, so when your friends or family read your cards, they will see the three arrows of the recycle symbol, reminding them to recycle themselves!

354 CHOOSE A HYBRID CAR

Hybrid cars are the first cars in 100 years that are actually lowering the noise pollution that cars make. If your parents are thinking of buying a new car, encourage them to consider a hybrid car. You could even do some of the research for them! Find out, in magazines and on the Internet, what kind of things hybrid cars can do to help the environment. Ask some of your classmates: Do any of their parents own a hybrid car? If so, how do they like it? Encourage them to tell you details that you can share with your parents, as part of your research.

Even if your parents are not planning on buying a new car soon, they can always go to a car dealership and take a hybrid car for a test drive. They can listen to what the salespeople have to say about hybrid cars, and maybe sometime in the future when your parents are thinking about buying a car, they will remember to look at hybrids or choose a car that has efficient gas mileage.

355 LEARN ABOUT: EPA

In 1970, the United States government formed the Environmental Protection Agency (EPA). The EPA was formed because people were demanding cleaner water, air, and land. Before that time, the government had no way to deal with the pollutants that were hurting people and the environment. The EPA began the hard work of trying to fix all the damage that had been done to the environment and by making new guidelines for Americans and U.S. businesses. Today, our Congress makes the laws that regulate the environment and the EPA makes sure people and businesses follow them.

356 SHARE THIS ECO-FACT: EPA ACTION

If people or businesses don't meet pollution standards, the EPA can take action against them. The EPA can help pay for environmental programs to study problems, clean them up, and educate the public so they can help too.

357 UNDERSTAND: SUPERFUND SITES

In 1982, the EPA set aside a lot of money to clean up places in the United States that had been damaged by the dumping of dangerous pollutants. These were called "superfund sites," because of the high cost of cleaning up the dangerous toxic pollutants. The EPA works with industries, businesses, state and local governments to:

- Stop pollution by lowering greenhouse gases, indoor air pollution, and toxic waste releases.
- Encourage the reuse of solid waste whenever possible.
- Identify and control pesticide risks.
- Discover new ways to save water and energy.

In return, the EPA encourages everyone to follow the rules by letting the public (you and me) know when a company is doing good environmental work. One of the most important goals of the EPA is to teach everyone how to be aware of, care for, and feel responsible for the environment. It is only through people knowing how and doing their part to take care of the earth that we can keep our environment safe for generations to come.

358 KEEP A NATURE JOURNAL

Express your love of nature by keeping a journal. Buy a decorated blank book, or just write in a plain notebook. Either way, make sure you like the journal and can carry it easily.

Find somewhere comfortable to do your writing. It can be under a backyard tree, on the front porch, or by a window with a pretty view. Perhaps you prefer a bench at the park or a sandy spot near the sea.

Take your journal along when you travel, too. Write about nature in different places.

You don't have to write a lot each time. Just write as much as you want. The idea is to have fun.

359 WHAT SHOULD YOU WRITE IN YOUR NATURE JOURNAL?

That's up to you! Here are some ideas to get you started:

- Describe the scene before you. What do you see? What sounds do you hear? What scents do you smell? Is it warm or cold? Is the air breezy or still?
- Focus on a single part of nature. What kind of tree are you sitting under? How does the grass feel and smell? How does the squirrel act as it scampers by?
- Find similes and metaphors in nature. A simile is a comparison using "like" or "as." For example: "The snow drifted against the fence like daubs of whipped cream." A metaphor says something is what you're comparing it to. For example: "The moss is a velvety green carpet on the forest floor."
- Find inspiration in nature. Sunlight outlining a dark cloud may make you feel hopeful. Dancing shadows of leaves may seem playful. Even a weed pushing through a sidewalk crack can show determination and a will to survive.

360 WRITE A NATURE HAIKU

What's a haiku, you might ask? It's a poem with seventeen total syllables. There should be five syllables in the first line, seven in the second, and five again in the third. Many poets have used haikus to express their feelings about nature. Go ahead and try to write one yourself—it's fun!

361 LEARN ABOUT HAIKUS!

Japanese haiku
Is a form of poetry.
Nature themes abound.

The form has three lines—
Five syllables, then seven,
Then just five again.

Count on your fingers.
Then it's easier to hear
Each word's syllables.

Paint a word picture.
Then add another image.
Where do they lead you?

Use visual clues,
Sounds, smells, and textures as well.
Bring the scene alive.

Write your own haiku.

Paint nature scenes with your words.

Share them with your friends.

362 SEE WHAT'S GOING ON IN THE REST OF THE WORLD

Want to learn even more about what you have read in this book? The Central Intelligence Agency (CIA) has a *World Factbook* online. This factbook includes data and information about every country in the world, including facts about the people, geography, and economics of each country. Go to the CIA's main website (*www.cia.gov*) and click on the link for *The World Factbook*. Saving our planet is world issue!

363 CHECK OUT THE NATIONAL GEOGRAPHIC SOCIETY WEBSITE

Learn about the world! You may be familiar with the well-known magazine *National Geographic*. This website (*www .nationalgeographic.com*) is produced and maintained by the same organization. At this site you will find information about different cultures, history, animals, and people from around the world. Go to the site and spend some time clicking around. You'll be amazed at what you find!

364 THINK OF THREE WAYS YOU CAN PERSONALLY USE LESS FOSSIL FUELS

Here's a challenge. Maybe you can walk or ride your bike to school instead of having your parents drive you. Maybe you can recycle your newspapers, cans, and bottles so they can be reused; this takes fewer fossil fuels than making materials from scratch. Take charge and look around your community for ways to help our planet!

365 USE THE FOUR R'S

Some day, the world will run out of oil. Some day, the world may run out of Bengal tigers. Some day, the world may even run out of clean water. But do you know what the world will never run out of? Do you know the one thing that is in unlimited supply? Knowledge.

Knowledge, and human willpower—the very same willpower that you have, as a living person, to say, "I can make a difference! And I'm going to do something!"

The choice to "go green" and live in an eco-friendly way is a decision we make every day, in ways both big and small. When you do one of the things identified in this book, you should feel very proud of yourself! Lots of people know we create a lot of our environment's problems, but not as many people actually do something about it!

You are important in the fight for the environment, and you can provide hope to future generations. The earth needs your help! Use the four R's:

- Reduce the amount of waste you and your family use
- Reuse materials
- Recycle those items you cannot reuse (also make sure you and your parents buy things that can be recycled)
- React by getting involved.

And most importantly . . . never stop believing that YOU are making a difference by living green!

MORE RESOURCES

Talk to your parents about contacting a "green group" or organization: You may find one in your community, you may find one online, or you may find information about one at an eco-fair or organic farm. Your Mom and Dad can help you figure out which organization you'd like to contact, and how to go about it. You could write, call, or send an e-mail through their website.

Organizations like these are always glad to hear from interested people like you. Not only will you get helpful information and statistics, you may also learn about activities, projects, classes you could take with your friends or family, or more ways to "go green" and help the environment. You may even make some new friends!

First, talk to your parents and tell them about your interest in finding out more about some of the things you've read about in this book. There are many, many groups out there doing good work.

Also talk to your parents before you go online to look at any websites, just to keep them informed about what you're interested in. Your parents can help you find even more resources on the Internet, and you know what? Your parents may end up learning a thing or two, too!

♻ The pages of this book are printed on 100% post-consumer recycled paper